The Future of the Overseas Chinese
in Southeast Asia

The Future
of the
Overseas Chinese
in Southeast Asia

LEA E. WILLIAMS

A VOLUME IN THE SERIES,
"THE UNITED STATES AND CHINA IN WORLD AFFAIRS"

PUBLISHED FOR THE COUNCIL ON FOREIGN RELATIONS BY THE

McGRAW-HILL BOOK COMPANY

New York · Toronto · London · Sydney

The Council on Foreign Relations is a non-profit institution devoted to the study of political, economic, and strategic problems as related to American foreign policy. It takes no stand, expressed or implied, on American policy.

The authors of books published under the auspices of the Council are responsible for their statements of fact and expressions of opinion. The Council is responsible only for determining that they should be presented to the public.

For my wife, Daisy Shen Williams

Foreword

This is the fourth volume in the series on The United States and China in World Affairs which is being sponsored by the Council on Foreign Relations through a generous grant from the Ford Foundation. In supporting this research program, the Council seeks to encourage more active and better informed consideration of one of the most important areas of foreign policy for the United States.

The Council program was under the able direction of Robert Blum until his untimely death, and it was he who envisaged the total project, arranged for the authors of the separate studies, and counseled them during the formative stages of their work. The appearance now of the completed studies constitutes appropriate memorials to his deep concern for a more enlightened public understanding of Asia.

This project, which has been guided by a Steering Committee under the chairmanship of Allen W. Dulles, has not sought to produce any single set of conclusions on a subject so complex as that of America's relations with China. Each study in the series therefore constitutes a separate and self-contained inquiry written on the responsibility of the author, who has reached his own judgments and conclusions regarding the subject of his investigations and its implications for U.S. policy. The list of authors includes persons with a variety of backgrounds in Chinese affairs and foreign policy. Some have had long personal experience in China. Others have studied China and Far Eastern problems during recent years or dealt with them as officials and administrators. They represent a variety of viewpoints and have, in each case, been able to consult with a group of qualified persons of diverse

vii

outlook whom the Council on Foreign Relations invited to meet with them periodically.

In this book, Professor Lea E. Williams surveys the present situation of the important Chinese populations of Southeast Asia and arrives at conclusions which should be of significance for U.S. policy. During the 1950s there was much concern over the degree to which the overseas Chinese in the new and fragile nations of Southeast Asia might serve as a fifth column for Communist China. It was widely assumed that the ultimate loyalties of these Chinese would be either to the mainland and Communist China or to Taiwan and Nationalist China. Few people were so bold as to believe that the overseas Chinese might become supporting citizens of their new homelands. Professor Williams suggests in this study, however, that in the mid-1960s the overseas Chinese are in fact displaying a capacity for assimilation into the life of the new countries and are not so engaged in the old politics of mainland Communists versus Taiwan-based Nationalists. Apparently, the cultural distinctiveness of the overseas Chinese was in part determined by the nature of colonial society, and with the ending of empire in Southeast Asia, the Chinese role has had to undergo profound changes. In describing the extent to which the Chinese are now seeking assimilation, particularly in Singapore and Malaysia, Professor Williams opens new prospects for constructive policy efforts.

Professor Williams, director of the Center for East Asian Studies at Brown University, has served in government, teaching, and research capacities in China and Southeast Asia: from 1944 to 1948 he was in the United States Foreign Service in China; in 1952–53 he was in Indonesia on a research team of the Center for International Studies of the Massachusetts Institute of Technology; from 1961 to 1963 he taught at the University of Singapore; and, as this study is published, he has returned to Southeast Asia for a year of further study.

LUCIAN W. PYE, Director
The United States and China in World Affairs

Preface

This survey is based on observations and conversations in Southeast Asia and elsewhere and on readings in the accessible literature. It seemed unnecessary to crowd the pages to follow with footnotes. Accordingly, only those sources quoted or referred to directly have been cited. A selected bibliography of the more useful works in English is appended.

The author is especially indebted to many of the writers listed in the bibliography and to the members of a study group assembled by the Council on Foreign Relations. This study group consisted of Edwin F. Stanton, chairman; James Basche, Harry J. Benda, Arnold Brackman, Rolland Bushner, Samuel B. Griffith, A. M. Halpern, William Henderson, Chang-tu Hu, Harold Isaacs, Arthur H. Rosen, G. William Skinner, Gerald Stryker, and Kenneth T. Young, Jr. Of course, any failings in this brief study, including those of interpretation, are the author's alone.

LEA E. WILLIAMS

Brown University
Providence, Rhode Island
May 1966

Contents

The Future of the Overseas Chinese
in Southeast Asia

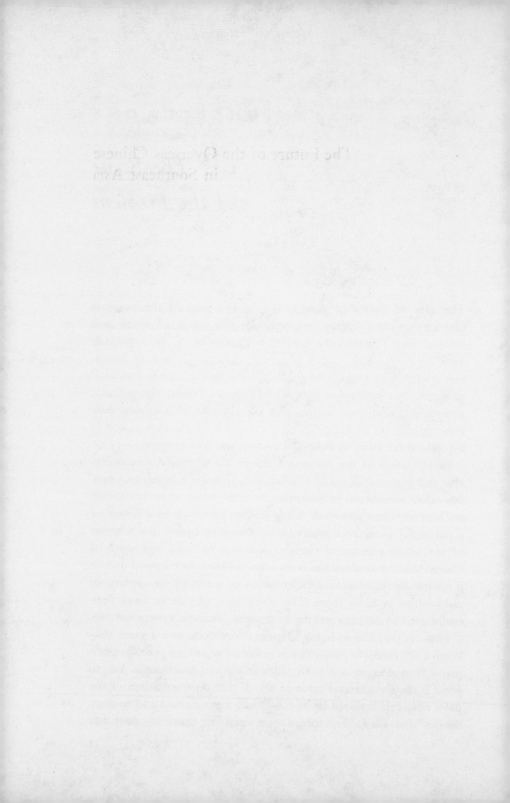

CHAPTER ONE

The Scene and the Problem

The fate of Southeast Asia is not in the grip of the overseas Chinese; on the contrary, the future of the overseas Chinese will be determined within the transitional societies of the region. It must be immediately added, however, that the Chinese of Southeast Asia possess great power and will not be mere passive participants in their history as it unfolds. For this reason, the political actions and economic decisions of the Chinese in Southeast Asia concern makers of policy in all the capitals of the region and in capitals as far away as Peking, London, and Washington.

Investigation of the overseas Chinese has occupied a considerable and growing corps of scholars and journalists in recent years. No other population in Southeast Asia has received such substantial and sustained attention. Some studies focus on the Chinese of a particular place or country; others seek to survey the Chinese of the whole expanse of tropical Asia east of India and south of China. Much fine work has been accomplished, but a good deal of nonsense has filled periodical columns or achieved the dignity of publication in book form. The worst sins, of course, have been committed by writers seeking to present dramatic generalizations.

Reports that the overseas Chinese are woven into a giant subversive net ready to paralyze and conquer Southeast Asia on command from Peking are both frightening and inaccurate. Yet so great is the commercial value of shock that representatives of the press have felt little shame at misleading their editors and readers. Stories that China has spread conspiratorial tentacles over her

3

southern neighbors have given just the right chill to many Sunday supplements.

The fact is that the overseas Chinese are anything but monolithic in their loyalties and orientations. Diversity, not uniformity, is their fundamental and most widespread quality. As time passes and as knowledge of this people expands, it becomes more and more difficult and dangerous to attempt to discuss the overseas Chinese as a unit. Hard though it is to draw parallels between peoples, it can be suggested that broad truths are almost as shallow for the overseas Chinese as for the overseas Europeans. Just as there is no real basis for treating as a unit for analysis peoples of European stock settled in California, Quebec, Chile, and South Africa, it is artificial and misleading to handle all Chinese abroad as an undifferentiated mass. The survey to follow will seek to emphasize the variety of the overseas Chinese and to stress that they are now in a process of quickened evolution.

Definition of "Overseas Chinese"

It is appropriate at this point to offer a definition and to set the limits of the discussion. The English term *overseas Chinese* is general and familiar; it is not altogether clear. The Chinese phrase *hua-ch'iao*, meaning Chinese sojourning abroad, is a bit more precise; but it is awkward and pedantic to employ it repeatedly in untranslated romanization. To a speaker of Chinese, *hua-ch'iao* are expatriates linked at least in a vague emotional way to China and in a more discernible manner to Chinese culture. The Chinese overseas have been regarded by recent Chinese governments as full members of China's political family. Until a short time ago the expatriates and all their descendants through the male line over infinite generations were officially classified as citizens of China. Every Chinese census or attempt at population count tallied the Chinese abroad as well as those within the state frontiers of China. Such official attachment to *jus sanguinis* was merely formal recognition of the force of the feeling of the overseas Chinese that together with Chinese in China they were *t'ung-pao*, children of the same womb. If "blood" were indeed a serviceable determinant of membership in the overseas Chinese people, the task of definition could be swiftly and neatly completed. The problem is far more elaborate.

No definition can be unfailingly sharp and concise because the decision on whether or not a man or a group is overseas Chinese is made by governments, both Chinese and foreign, by the larger societies alongside and within which Chinese settlers live, and by innumerable individuals. One thing is certain: overseas Chinese identification depends far more on personal social attitudes than on official legislation.

Several attributes can be listed as those of the overseas Chinese. Chinese ancestry, at least on the father's side, is clearly essential. Birth in China is by no means a basic requirement; indeed, today most overseas Chinese were born far from their ancestral villages. Foreign residence must be extended or permanent. A Chinese student, diplomat, or merchant away from China for a specific purpose and definite period is not an overseas Chinese. In recent years, a new type of Chinese expatriate, the political refugee, has appeared in many places; but such a person is not necessarily an overseas Chinese either. The exclusion of a major percentage of the refugees is due in part to the fact that their emigration was not prompted by a wish to settle abroad in search of economic well-being and in part to provincial and class considerations. A great number of those who fled China as a result of the establishment of Communist power there are from areas other than the southeastern provinces which historically produced the emigrant Chinese. A gap in language and tradition separates many of these refugees from north or central China from the overseas people of southern origin; furthermore, the overseas Chinese have adopted much from the cultures of their countries of residence and have, to the refugees, become semi-Chinese. Possibly more instrumental in the maintenance of the separation is the fact that the refugees by and large consider themselves people of superior status. As holders of university degrees, as former officials, as professional men, the refugees apparently see little basis for social communion with plebeian compatriots.

The difficulty of determining a man's membership in the overseas Chinese people is compounded by the fact that individual attitudes are of central relevance. A person who considers him-

self an overseas Chinese and is accepted as such by the Chinese and
by the non-Chinese in his area clearly qualifies. More troublesome
is the man who lives in spirit between the overseas Chinese and the
indigenous populations. Many persons of Chinese ancestry are
now in a transitional state between overseas Chinese identity and
assimilation. There are those who rarely think of their Chinese
ancestry and are not now overseas Chinese but who could be
pushed into active Chinese identification by the refusal of the
governments and indigenous peoples of their overseas homelands
to permit the absorption of ethnic Chinese into the nation. On the
reverse side of this slippery coin, men who now have only limited
awareness of overseas Chinese connections could be drawn toward
final assimilation with the more deeply rooted peoples of Southeast
Asia. Both processes have historical precedent. In the past, some
Chinese have disappeared into the Southeast Asian masses, while
others have been pushed back from the brink of assimilation.

For what it may be worth, a working definition can be submitted: an overseas Chinese is a person of some Chinese ancestry
who views residence abroad as compatible with Chinese cultural
identity and less certainly with some remote Chinese political orientation. The overseas Chinese considers his expatriation the
result of his own or his forebears' economic strivings. He regards
himself as a member of the overseas Chinese people, which is,
in turn, part of the greater Chinese nation, and is so regarded by
those around him.

The definition offered is anything but foolproof; it rests on too
many intangibles. Perhaps the sense of it will become clearer as
this study develops. As a final observation, it can be mentioned
that the overseas Chinese are roughly similar to the *pieds noirs* of
Algeria, who claimed French identity although they were often
generations removed from Europe, or to those New Zealanders
who on occasion speak of England as home.

Overseas Chinese Not Confined to Southeast Asia

Although this study is concerned exclusively with Southeast Asia,
it must not be assumed that other parts of the world are without

overseas Chinese residents. India, Japan, Korea, Australia, Oceania, South Africa, Madagascar, and of course the Americas have large and established communities of this people. Many cities of northwestern Europe boast their Chinatowns. Other areas have received only scattered immigrants, but it is rare to discover a country without isolated Chinese settlers or their heirs. There was recently, for example, but a lone Chinese established in Liberia; more happily, there were three in Norway, who may have kept each other company.[1] Parenthetically, it should be noted that the Chinese of Hong Kong have been designated overseas Chinese by some sources, including Chinese governments, but that that population does not fit within any realistic definition of overseas Chinese. The majority of Hong Kong inhabitants appear to consider themselves residents of a segment of their native Kwangtung province which happens to be under the British flag. It should be kept in mind, however, that Hong Kong is as close to China as most overseas Chinese travelers get these days and is a center for overseas investment. Hong Kong also sets much of the style in fashion and entertainment for the Chinese abroad.

Passing observations on the communities of the Americas may indicate the high level of adaptability of the overseas Chinese. In the United States in the middle decades of the nineteenth century, most Chinese immigrants first found employment as manual laborers in railroad construction and mining in the Far West. The name "Old Gold Mountain," now used for San Francisco but formerly applied by some to all of the United States known to the immigrants, is a clear reflection of the motives of the Chinese who arrived in California and neighboring areas in the early days. When the labor shortage in the West was ended by an influx of Irish and native American workers, pressures on the Chinese built up. The enactment of federal curbs on immigration was an official expression of resentment. Less formally, Chinese workers were forced out of occupations in which they competed with men of European origin. By the beginning of the present century, the Chinese coming to the United States were obliged to resort to inventive subterfuge to slip through the barriers of the Exclusion

[1] *Chung-hua min-kuo nien-chien* [*Republic of China Yearbook*] (Taipei: Chung-hua min-kuo nien-chien she, 1961), pp. 329–330.

Act. Once in the country, the new arrivals could only join earlier immigrants in performing tasks scorned by others. They worked as servants, cooks, waiters, and most ubiquitously as laundrymen. Huddled in Chinatowns, where men outnumbered women many times over, the immigrants toiled to save for a return to China. Gambling was their chief recreation; for some, the possibility of winning offered the only hope for escape from a drab and degrading existence. The Chinese of those years made little imprint on American society. Only when secret society murders or traffic in narcotics invited police attention did the general American public give much thought to the Chinese in their midst.

No broad change in this bleak picture was to come until World War II. Men could spend their entire adult lives in America without learning more than a few words of English having largely to do with laundry tickets. Indeed, there were even some Chinatown citizens born in the United States who never fully mastered English. Contact between the Chinese and others was restricted almost to the point of meaninglessness. But a new pattern was soon to take shape.

The war years had a special impact on the Chinese of the United States. China was an ally, so old prejudices became unpatriotic. More important, many younger men left the Chinatowns to serve in the American armed forces or to work in war industries. In 1943, the Exclusion Act was repealed; and though the new quota of 105 Chinese immigrants a year was primarily of symbolic rather than real significance, the end of exclusion enabled a substantial number of Chinese-American veterans to bring brides from China. More recent legislation has since provided for family reunification and the admission of political refugees. As family life of the kind Americans normally seek is awkward in jammed and often blighted Chinatown neighborhoods, the younger generation of Chinese-Americans, along with millions of others, began to move to the suburbs. In addition, men no longer sought the traditional and menial occupations. More and more, the Chinatowns have become business centers where the daytime populations are far greater than those of the night, when aging bachelors are the chief residents. The Chinese of the United States, then, in the past quarter of a century have moved rapidly toward cultural assimilation. As the most recent example of the working of the American melting pot, the Chinese case is exciting; but Americanization takes Chinese-Americans out of the world of overseas Chinese politics.

Chinese settlers in Latin America were permitted to begin the process of assimilation earlier than their fellows in the United States. Brought in great numbers to Peru and Cuba in the nineteenth century to labor in mining and agriculture, the early Chinese immigrants experienced dreadful hardships. Many perished under conditions usually associated only with the cruelest slavery. In actual fact, the Chinese were often mere surrogates for emancipated slaves.

Starting from generally more humble positions than those filled by Chinese in the United States in the post-Civil War decades, the Chinese of Latin America rose rather rapidly to middle-class status. Opportunities opened in retail trade in Peru, Cuba, Mexico, Colombia, and elsewhere. Many Latin American Chinese came to fill intermediate economic and social positions between the European elites and the Indian or Negro masses. The pattern, as will be shown later, was parallel to that which transformed Southeast Asia. Being placed in a comfortable middle-class niche, the Chinese of Latin America have not shared the urge of the Chinese in the postwar United States to lose themselves in the larger society; but, living in racially flexible societies, the Latin American Chinese have long been moving toward assimilation through intermarriage. Thus, the Chinese in the United States are presently shedding their economic and social distinctiveness, while Chinese south of the Rio Grande are tending to disappear in a physical sense.

Despite the near ubiquitousness of Chinese overseas, it is necessary and appropriate to restrict the scope of this present effort to a treatment of that people in Southeast Asia. It is only in that region that the overseas Chinese are a force of consequence. Furthermore, as Southeast Asia is a scene of developing confrontation between the United States and the People's Republic of China, the Chinese settlers there are subjects of timely and compelling concern.

Distribution of Overseas Chinese in Southeast Asia

Although all definitions of overseas Chinese are arbitrary and although census data for Southeast Asia tend strongly to be imaginative, it remains instructive to consider figures on the populations of the region and the percentage of Chinese in them. (See Table 1-1.) As the numbers are based on more than one source and in part on the present writer's guesswork, they have been rounded off for the sake of convenience and to stress their conjectural nature.

A foreign visitor to Southeast Asia unfamiliar with population estimates of the kind produced here would be likely to conclude that the number of Chinese is vastly greater than it is in fact. The overseas Chinese are so highly urbanized that many of the towns and cities seen by outsiders are heavily Chinese in population and atmosphere. Even in places where the Chinese form but a small minority of the urban residents, their numbers seem great because of their concentration in the chief commercial neighborhoods and along the main traffic arteries. In this shallow sense, the Chinese patterns of urban settlement mislead the passing observer. In political and economic terms, however, the urbanization and concentration of the Chinese are measures of their power and vitality. If the less than 6 per cent of the Southeast Asian peoples with Chinese roots were evenly distributed geographically and occupationally throughout the rural and urban districts of the region, the overseas Chinese would exercise insignificant influence and attract only limited notice. Under those circumstances, there would surely be no need for this study.

Chinese settlers are most numerous in those parts of Southeast Asia where economic development has created a need for their energies and an opportunity for the application of their talents and where administrative policies on immigration have been hospitable. The Chinese settled, in other words, where they were tolerated and where their resources could be developed. They were attracted by the prospect of economic growth, and they

TABLE 1-1. Number and Percentage of Overseas Chinese
in the Populations of Southeast Asia

	Number of Ethnic Chinese	Total Population	Percentage of Chinese
Brunei	25,000	95,000	26.3
Burma	400,000 a	25,300,000	1.6
Cambodia	435,000	6,250,000	7.0
Indonesia	2,750,000	106,000,000	2.6
Laos	45,000	2,100,000	2.1
Malaysia	3,315,000	9,435,000	35.1
Malaya	[2,920,000]	[8,090,000]	[36.1]
Sarawak	[275,000]	[830,000]	[32.5]
Sabah (formerly British North Borneo)	[120,000]	[515,000]	[23.3]
Philippines	450,000	32,100,000	1.4
Portuguese Timor	5,000	575,000	.9
Singapore	1,400,000	1,880,000	74.5
Thailand	2,600,000	30,500,000	8.5
North Vietnam	190,000 b	18,400,000	1.0
South Vietnam	860,000	16,300,000	5.3
Total	12,475,000	248,835,000	5.0

ᵃ As an untallied but presumably substantial number of Chinese have ille-
gally crossed the border into Burma, figures for that country are especially
uncertain.

ᵇ U.N. figures indicate that this many *Hoa* people are in North Vietnam.
As no "Chinese" are listed and as *Hoa* is a Vietnamese term for Chinese,
Skinner has concluded that the Chinese population of the country is 190,000.
This is an unusually high figure.

Sources: Chung-hua min-kuo nien-chien [*Republic of China Yearbook*]
(Taipei: Chung-hua min-kuo nien-chien she, 1961), pp. 327–328; *Chugoku
no keizai-kensetsu to Kakyo* [*China's Economic Development and the
Overseas Chinese*] (Tokyo: Ajiya Keizai-kenkysuho, 1960), p. 8; *Malaysia in Brief* (Kuala Lumpur: Department of Information, 1963), p. 8; Statistical Office of the United Nations, Department of Economic and Social
Affairs, *Demographic Yearbook, 1963* (15th ed.; New York: Author, 1964),
passim; Statistical Office of the United Nations, "Population and Vital
Statistics Report," *Statistical Papers*, Series A, v. 16, no. 3, 1964, *passim;
The New York Times,* October 21, 1964.
    G. William Skinner has compiled estimates on Southeast Asia's Chinese
population as of mid-1965. I have gratefully used his figures in drawing up
the table presented here.

stimulated development. Since economic growth has taken place by and large in those cities and towns where commerce and light industry have prospered and in those places where estate agriculture and mining have succeeded, the massive concentrations of overseas Chinese are to be found in great cities such as Singapore, Jakarta, Saigon, Bangkok, and Manila and in countless smaller places with less familiar but more exotic names such as Klang, Sibu, Cheribon, or Zamboango. Other areas of thick Chinese settlement are found in tin-mining districts such as those of the states of Perak and Selangor in Malaya or on the Indonesian islands of Bangka and Billiton, in the rubber estate areas of Malaya, and in similarly developed areas on Sumatra and Borneo.

The relatively small percentage of Chinese in Burma and the Philippines, where starts toward economic development were made decades ago, is to be explained by the obstacles to Chinese immigration which existed in those two countries. Under British rule, Burma was administered as part of the Indian Empire until not long before World War II. As a result, the Indians were encouraged to move into Burma to take up many of the positions in the economy which were coming to be held by Chinese elsewhere in Southeast Asia. The Indians simply got into Burma before the Chinese. The Philippine picture is the result of conscious efforts by generations of Spanish and American officials to check Chinese immigration. The historical record of the modern Philippines before the twentieth century reveals an enduring Spanish fear of Chinese competition. After 1898, the Americans applied the principles of their own policy of Chinese exclusion to their Southeast Asian colony. Filipino political figures were generally enthusiastic in their support of that feature of American rule.

As a final point, it must be observed that there are tens of thousands of exceptions to the rule placing the overseas Chinese in urban centers or in regions of large-scale mining and agricultural enterprises. Chinese peasants are established in numbers in places where there is a demand for their specialization in the raising of garden vegetables, swine, and poultry. The countryside around the cities with markets for the products of Chinese gardening skill is often intensively and lovingly tended. In Thai-

land and Malaya, Chinese gardens and farms are especially conspicuous. Another type of Chinese farm, once particularly common in postwar Malaya, is that of the squatter, the man who seeks
to win a subsistence livelihood from land to which he holds no title
on the fringes of settled districts. Finally, in Sarawak and Sabah
many Chinese farms produce export crops for the world market.
Although the Chinese peasantry of Southeast Asia probably
represent no more than 5 per cent of the total overseas Chinese
population, the support sought of the farmers by insurrectionists
in Malaya during the early years of the 1948–60 Emergency and
in Sarawak during the recent terrorism there has caused realistic
alarm.

The Present Situation and Future Prospects
of the Overseas Chinese in Southeast Asia

The past few years have been a time of turmoil for the overseas
Chinese. Changes and challenges have come with growing frequency. The times have been so demanding and unsettling that
the overseas Chinese themselves are confused in response and
apprehensive of the future. It is more than a little foolhardy for
an outsider to attempt to examine the overseas Chinese in their
present condition of uncertainty and upheaval, yet the study
offered here will seek to define the dimensions of the problem.

The process of rapid change for the overseas people began with
the early stirring of their national consciousness at the end of the
last century. Before that awakening, the Chinese attachments of
the immigrants were based on kinship and culture. By the time of
the overthrow of the Manchu dynasty in 1911, however, the
overseas settlers had become a mobilized and major driving force
in the Chinese nationalist revolution. Chinese nationalism, an
intense feeling of active, intimate, political attachment to China,
became the faith and hope of the overseas people. The feeling
grew as the twentieth century moved on and reached a peak during the Japanese attack on China from 1937. In the postwar years,
the force of overseas Chinese nationalism has been dissipated by

the contending and shifting claims for loyalty of the Communists and the Nationalists and, as will be made clear in later chapters, by the nascent realization that Southeast Asia, not China, is home.

Close on the heels of the overseas Chinese nationalist upsurge came that of the Southeast Asian host nations. Beginning in the Philippines in the final Spanish years, nationalism inspired and transformed the peoples of the region. By the eve of the Japanese conquest, Southeast Asian nationalist energies tested the skill and tried the patience of colonial administrators virtually everywhere; the wartime destruction of the colonial order was irreparable. In little more than a decade after the war, nationalist revolution triumphed in country after country. By 1957, mere anachronistic fragments of empire remained under British, Dutch, or Portuguese authority. In the years since, all but the Portuguese on their half of Timor have lowered the imperial flags.

All the nationalist revolutions, each transfer of sovereignty from Western to Southeast Asian hands, challenged the overseas Chinese. As a minority people and as workers and entrepreneurs whose survival depends upon the economic health of their host countries, the Chinese were fearful of the chaos of revolution and reconstruction. Their apprehension was compounded by the fact that suspicion of the Chinese is endemic throughout the region and hostility toward them is virulent among many local nationalists.

The growth of the Chinese Communist colossus on the northern horizon has confronted the overseas Chinese with yet another set of challenges. In addition to the question of whether overseas Chinese nationalist ardor was to be directed toward Peking or Taipei, the settlers faced the problem of having their schools, press, labor unions, virtually all their interests manipulated by one or both of the contenders. Equally threatening to many has been the fact that some Southeast Asian leaders and governments have put pressure on the overseas Chinese and their organizations to curb communism or simply to establish their own political respectability. A Singapore Chinese cliché sums up the danger with telling irony: "To be anti-Communist is to be anti-Chinese; to be anti-Chinese is to be a true anti-Communist."

Apart from, but interacting with, the storms generated by communism, the now familiar revolution of rising expectations has engulfed the overseas Chinese from two directions. First, the overseas Chinese themselves have been stirred by this worldwide revolution; indeed, it could be argued that immigrants from China brought it to Southeast Asia. Today among the overseas Chinese, the struggles of unionized labor, the aggressiveness of students, the acquisitiveness of petty traders, and the boldness of capital point to active participation in the revolution. Second, the new economic goals and material desires of the indigenous Southeast Asians are coming increasingly to match and compete with those of the overseas Chinese. Not so long ago, in a more relaxed time, Indonesians and Filipinos or others mixed admiration and jealousy in their view of Chinese prosperity. Recently, the reaction has taken on the more positive form of seeking means to check Chinese advance and overtake it. Economic nationalism is a tide throughout the region. As the overseas Chinese raise their own sights, their locally-rooted neighbors prepare to contest every Chinese gain.

As the final third of this century opens, the Chinese of Southeast Asia find themselves in an unprecedented state of anxiety. They are compelled to respond to contending nationalist forces, to communism, to revolutions, to economic chauvinism, and to the shock waves set up by power-bloc struggles. The insecurity of the overseas Chinese endangers political stability and stunts economic growth in all the countries of the region. The menace of political extremism, both Chinese and indigenous, is nurtured by anti-Chinese discrimination and violence. Fear of official hostility or of mob attack prevents some Chinese entrepreneurs from making full use of their talents and their capital. Governments could be overthrown by the forces of lawlessness and the economic sickness thus produced. As U.S. policy objectives in Southeast Asia call for the attainment of political viability and the stimulation of material advance, the plight and future of the overseas Chinese ought to concern thoughtful Americans. Although the United States can take only peripheral part in the actions which will help determine the overseas Chinese course, the solution of the difficulties of that people would be clearly in the American interest.

Unless the People's Republic of China dominates settlement of the issue through open military conquest or massive and successful subversion, the place of the overseas Chinese in Southeast Asia will be determined within the region. In independent Southeast Asia, the opportunities for the social, political, and economic accommodation of the overseas Chinese with the indigenous and ruling majority seem to be expanding. If it can be assumed that the region has time to carry the process of political assimilation well along toward completion, there are genuine and substantial bases for optimism; but in human history, time is grudgingly allotted. On this note of guarded and hedged hope, it is time to move on.

The balance of this study will first survey the social, economic, and political circumstances of the overseas Chinese and then trace the historical development of the current environment. Resting on those foundations, the examination will assess aspects of the policies of the Nationalists on Taiwan and the Communists on the mainland toward Chinese communities abroad. The central thesis to be offered will be presented in a chapter on change among the overseas Chinese; the emphasis will be on trends toward local political assimilation and away from chauvinism and communalism. The final chapter will deal with considerations for U.S. policy.

CHAPTER TWO

Overseas Chinese Diversity, Assets, and Handicaps

To understand the Chinese of Southeast Asia, it is essential to recognize their diversity, yet this aspect of the overseas Chinese has been long and distressingly ignored. Actually, nineteenth-century writers were in a sense more perceptive than many of their twentieth-century heirs have been. Until nationalism began to generate forces for unification of the overseas Chinese some six decades ago, treatments of the Chinese settlers laid heavy stress on the linguistic boundaries dividing the immigrants into recognizable groups of Cantonese, Hainanese, Fukienese, and so on. Some early writers even went to the extreme of referring to the language communities as tribes; beyond that, however, there was a general failure to appreciate overseas Chinese diversity. Once nationalism gained hold, the Chinese abroad were most often viewed as a bloc of aliens with grasping economic ambitions and sinister political goals. At present, there seems to be an increasing awareness of overseas Chinese heterogeneity, although quite recently a book on Thailand presented the unsupportable and whimsical notion that Chinese society there lacks a class structure.

Diversities

The diversity of the overseas Chinese can be seen in a number of areas. The matter of language is most easily discussed. The variety of the home languages in current use is more than a little remarkable. The several South China tongues native to the immigrants of course survive and serve a majority of the Chinese households of Southeast Asia. In this century, the success of education in what is normally known in English as Mandarin, the official national language of China, has encouraged many younger overseas Chinese to adopt that language for daily use. In families where husband and wife are from different language backgrounds, Mandarin is sometimes used within the home, and children may grow up knowing no other Chinese tongue.

The list of languages spoken in overseas Chinese families does not end with those brought south from China by ancestors in earlier times or by Mandarin teachers in the more recent past. All the major and several of the minor Southeast Asian languages and dialects are employed. In some cases, the overseas Chinese have developed their own dialects of Southeast Asian languages. The most fully studied example of this phenomenon is the Sino-Malay spoken for generations by the so-called Baba Chinese in Malacca and on a more limited scale elsewhere in Malaya. With varying degrees of purity, many Chinese throughout Southeast Asia rely on languages native to the region for their daily needs at home. Tens of thousands of overseas Chinese children grow up fully assimilated linguistically to, say, the Thai or the Indonesian majorities among whom they live.

Finally, the languages of the former colonial rulers have been adopted by some of the Western-educated Chinese of Southeast Asia. There are many families, especially in the upper economic strata, where English, Dutch, or French is used exclusively in the home. Members may know no Chinese at all and only enough of the local indigenous language to communicate with servants and tradespeople.

In the matter of language, then, the overseas Chinese are anything but unified. Recognition of the close links between language and thought and behavior leads to the conclusion that the political actions of the overseas Chinese are not likely to be uniform.

As with language, the customs of the overseas Chinese display colorful variety. Levels of acculturation differ widely. There are a few whose manner of living appears little changed from the mode of ancestral villages in China; at the other extreme are pockets of Chinese who are virtually indistinguishable from the local indigenous peoples. Settlers seemingly untouched by the impact of immigration are rare, and settlements of Chinese wholly acculturated to the Southeast Asian environment are even rarer. Nevertheless, both phenomena can be discovered. The great bulk of the overseas Chinese, needless to say, find themselves in intermediate stages of acculturation. Even without the revolutionary transformation of China in the last fifteen years, almost all overseas Chinese would feel in part alien in the land of their own or their ancestors' birth. Correspondingly, the overseas Chinese, with few exceptions, would feel strange if fully thrust into the indigenous cultures of their host countries. The overseas Chinese have, in other words, developed cultures or subcultures of their own.

Overseas Chinese cultural patterns are woven of many threads —Chinese, Southeast Asian, and Western. One family may eat Javanese curry with chopsticks, while another uses European tableware to eat Cantonese sweet and sour pork. Elaborate feasts may be enlivened by toasts in cognac. The rituals attending birth, marriage, and death have all felt the force of cultural change and innovation. Shifts away from traditional Chinese usage are most readily seen in preferences for Western clothing for men, children, and many women or those for architectural improvisation drawing upon local as well as external inspiration.

Religion is another area in which change has come to and been wrought by the overseas Chinese. In addition to the erosion of religious customs presumably inevitable among uprooted immigrants, an infusion of practices from outside sources has taken place. The syncretic Buddhism of Chinese settlers reaching Burma, Thailand, or Cambodia was rather effortlessly altered and even replaced by the Theravada Buddhist faith of those countries. Less to be anticipated is the adoption by the Chinese in Malaysia and Indonesia of some of the beliefs and practices, both Muslim and animist, of the indigenous people, although conversion to Islam has been singularly uncommon.

Finally, overseas Chinese settlements have long been fields of Christian missionary endeavor. Particularly in colonies where proselytism flourished, communities of Christian Chinese achieved moderate size and considerable influence. Both because of the advantages of missionary schooling and because of the religious connection with the Western ruling stratum, the Chinese Christians came to enjoy positions of prestige and power not warranted by their numbers. Protestant and Roman Catholic Chinese are scattered throughout the region, with Catholics understandably more numerous where the French, Portuguese, or Spanish have ruled.

Diversity is no doubt clearest to the transient observer who takes note of the infinite variety of occupations and the economic-class spectrum running from crushing misery to incalculable wealth. One stereotype of the Southeast Asian Chinese is of a sleek, affluent merchant guided by industrious habits and flexible ethics. The commercial life of his adopted land is thought to be in the grip of men like himself who are supposed to be selfishly and ruthlessly engaged in exploitation. It is the belief of many, perhaps most, indigenous Southeast Asians that the Chinese in their midst contribute nothing but extract much. Economic jealousy has deep and extensive roots.

It is beyond dispute that a huge share of the trade of Southeast Asia goes through Chinese hands. The thought of commerce in most of the region suddenly without the Chinese is preposterous— like the idea of an army ordered to fight only with left-handed soldiers. Nevertheless, it is false to believe that the overseas Chinese are exclusively or even usually great merchants. For every overseas Chinese commercial giant, there are thousands of petty traders, and for every small shopkeeper or itinerant peddler, there are scores of laborers. Furthermore, there are overseas Chinese in almost every occupation, skilled or unskilled, manual or intellectual, lucrative or subsistence. Chinese work as servants, stevedores, sailors, and surgeons, as rubber tappers, radio announcers, race-track touts, and real-estate brokers. There is probably not an occupation without Chinese representation, although in Southeast Asia as a whole relatively few Chinese pursue political, bureaucratic, or military careers. Positions in those governmental fields have historically been held by colonial expatriates and their indigenous personnel, except in Thailand, and are now everywhere all but monopolized by Southeast Asians of local origin. Laws to prevent Chinese participation in some occupations are in force in some areas, but the broad picture of occupational diversity remains valid.

The point to emphasize here is that despite the popular indigenous belief that most settlers are merchants, the overseas Chinese display no economic-class cohesiveness. The largest of their occupational groups is composed of men in trade, but that body is far from united as an interest group. Its membership includes at one extreme men who sell one cigarette at a time to customers too poor to afford more and at the other end men who deal in tons of rubber and tin on the world market. The Chinese of Southeast Asia, because such a weighty percentage are in trade, ought logically to be model bourgeois; they are not. Their class interests, loyalties, and identifications are manifold; their political convictions are far from solid.

Since the Communist victory in China in 1949, efforts to assess the political inclinations of the overseas Chinese have been numerous and rather consistently fruitless. Some analysts have concluded that backing for Peking is massive and disciplined; others have argued that the Chinese abroad form a vast real or potential reservoir of support for the Nationalists on Taiwan. Parenthetically, it should be mentioned that the assumed political opportunism of the overseas Chinese has been cited as an argument against American recognition of the People's Republic of China. The theory is that such a diplomatic shift would cause the Chinese of Southeast Asia to topple off the political fence and into the arms of Peking.

A popular journalistic appraisal of the political attachments of the Chinese in Southeast Asia has achieved wide and perhaps justified currency. Ten per cent of the overseas Chinese, according to this estimate, are pro-Communist; another 10 per cent are sympathetic to the Nationalists; and the remaining 80 per cent seek to avoid open commitment. Possibly the shrewdest evaluation in the experience of the present writer was offered by a man not claiming specialization in the subject who expressed the simple thought that the overseas Chinese appear fundamentally pro-overseas Chinese. Once that view is accepted, however, there remains the formidable task of examining the ways in which the overseas Chinese have sought and seek to serve their own peculiar individual and collective interests.

Each overseas Chinese is of course shaped politically by his family, circle of friends, class, economic interests and education. He is also guided by the actions of the government of his host country and by those of the governments in Peking and Taipei. Most elusively, the pressures of his own personality bear on his political behavior. There can be no short, definite answer to the question of why one man swings over to the Communists, another is pro-Nationalist, a third displays loyalty to his Southeast Asian homeland, and a fourth appears apathetic and apolitical.

The difficulties met in attempts to study the political orientation of the overseas Chinese are due not only to the variety of loyalties and the manner of their expression but also to the fact that it is necessary for many persons to appear politically withdrawn. Communist sympathies must be concealed in some countries; open support for the Nationalists is impossible in others. In all Southeast Asia, only Malaysia and Singapore permit the Chinese to be conspicuous politically as a people; and even there organized political identification with the governments or parties of Taiwan or the China mainland is banned. Understandably, the overseas Chinese are secretive in matters of political ideology. There is no direct and simple way for the political scientist to measure loyalties by taking polls, although naïve efforts at such data gathering have been attempted. Not long ago, for example, an enthusiastic young American arrived in the area equipped with a lengthy questionnaire to present to sample overseas Chinese. He hoped that people would disclose preference for or rejection of Communist Chinese books, periodicals, radio broadcasts, and films. Inquiry was also to discover whether or not ties were maintained with the China mainland through letters, remittances, and travel. To the surprise of no one except the frustrated pollster, neat techniques were inapplicable. Sophisticated survey research can be rewarding and enlightening, but overseas Chinese political views must in part be ascertained through inference and informed intuition. Facts can be assembled on voting where the franchise is established, on educational preferences, on decisions between

Southeast Asian and Chinese citizenship, on labor union and other mass-organization activities, and on more subtle signs of political orientation. Interpretation of the facts, however, can only be individual and provisional. For this reason, assessments of the overseas Chinese reach contending conclusions.

Assets and Handicaps

Although it is necessary to highlight the diversity of the Chinese abroad, it is still useful to offer certain general observations on characteristics shared in large measure by the overseas Chinese as a people. These can perhaps most conveniently be put in the form of a balance sheet of overseas Chinese strengths and weaknesses. The credit side of the ledger is more widely known and can be opened first.

Assets. In literacy and education, the overseas Chinese stand above the other peoples of Southeast Asia. Among the older, China-born settlers, illiteracy was the rule rather than the exception; but their heirs have reversed the situation. It is growing uncommon, indeed extraordinary, to meet a young Chinese unable to read and write his ancestral language or that of his tropical homeland. Beyond the simple attainment of literacy, many Chinese in the area go on to secondary school and a significant minority reach university level. The government universities in Malaysia and Singapore are heavily Chinese in enrollment; elsewhere in Southeast Asia, Chinese students, although prevented by discriminatory quota systems from constituting a majority, are conspicuous both in numbers and achievement on virtually every campus. The proportion of overseas Chinese seeking advanced and professional education abroad is considerably greater than that of indigenous Southeast Asians. Relative prosperity, the traditional Chinese respect and hunger for learning, urbanization, and the establishment of the overseas Chinese in occupations valuing education have created these circumstances.

The acquisition of education is of course an idle exercise if the skills and learning mastered are not put to use. Not only do the

Chinese of Southeast Asia apply their education in obvious ways in the earning of livelihoods, but their high literacy rate permits them to be the best-informed people in the area. Newspapers and other publications reach the Chinese in great quantity and with regularity. Figures on newspaper circulation broken down to indicate the ethnic backgrounds of subscribers are not available, yet it is known that a substantial proportion of the mass-circulation papers in the area are Chinese in language or ownership. As an example, the most popular and responsibly objective daily in Indonesia, until it was suppressed, was a Chinese paper published in both Chinese and Indonesian editions. Although the proportion may be smaller, it would not be unreasonable to guess that close to half of all the newspapers distributed in Southeast Asia go to the Chinese 5 or 6 per cent of the total population.

Less formal channels of communication are also open to the Chinese. Through travel and correspondence, the Chinese of one community keep in touch with those of other settlements in the area. It would be instructive to assemble figures on the flow of mail among the Chinese. Such data are not at hand, but it can be assumed that Chinese, who rank so high both in literacy and in commerce, contribute highly to the volume of mail in Southeast Asia. With respect to communication through travel, even cursory observation of travel facilities in the region reveals that Chinese move around a great deal. Correspondence and visits between friends, relatives, and business associates enable the Chinese to maintain links among themselves within the region and beyond. Similarly, within a community, the Chinese keep informed through personal and business ties and through their associations. In short, the overseas Chinese have far more access to information than their indigenous neighbors. Horizons broadened initially through emigration have been further expanded through both formal and informal channels of communication. The concerns and interests of most Southeast Asians seemingly do not normally extend beyond the village; the more urbanized, educated, and affluent Chinese are much better placed to be aware of national and international developments. The simple fact that so many overseas Chinese are engaged in business and must keep up with political trends and trade shifts necessitates wakefulness.

The chief resource of the overseas people, their energy, is a most unwieldy subject to discuss. Simple and final explanations for overseas Chinese drive are not to be found. Nobody denies that the Chinese of Southeast Asia are the outstandingly industrious and productive people there, but there has been no full analysis of the reasons for this behavior. Perhaps there never can be. In any case, the social scientist who may seek to account for overseas Chinese energy will have to be both sophisticated and bold. To date, a number of partial explanations of the phenomenon have been offered.

It has been pointed out that the Chinese emigrants who entered Southeast Asia typically sought to save for eventual, ideally early, retirement and repatriation. Industry and frugality were joined to make possible the attainment of the goal of a return to China. Related to this explanation is the theory that the demands of the traditional Chinese family system imposed a burden of productivity on expatriate members. Remittances from abroad to relatives in South China villages were tangible expressions of family loyalty. The legacy of generations of peasant thrift and toil is also supposed to have endowed the Chinese emigrants with endurance and strength. Furthermore, Southeast Asia was a land of unknown opportunity to Chinese peasant emigrants, who made the most of avenues to success closed in their crowded and socially stratified ancestral homeland.

Among the overseas Chinese themselves, a climatic explanation of their energy is often heard. It is believed that the cycle of seasons in China generates habits of industry alien to natives of the monotonous tropics. Embroidering upon this theory, some go on to state that Chinese born in Southeast Asia appear to be lethargic in comparison with their China-born ancestors and compatriots. There may, in fact, be a real basis for this theory, for it is indeed hard to maintain a compelling sense of time where the climate is changeless.

Finally, some observers, both Chinese and Western and presumably equally unreliable, attribute overseas Chinese dynamism to heredity. Racial explanations of behavior, while discredited scientifically, are sadly far from unfashionable in lay circles. It is not rare to encounter overseas Chinese convinced that their genes deserve all the credit. Such men are likely to seek to put the capstone on the argument by pointing out that people of mixed Chinese and indigenous ancestry display many of the relaxed qualities of their local forebears. Sometimes the climatic and genetic explanations are paired.

Whatever the truth may be, the Chinese of Southeast Asia are as a people uniquely industrious. More significant than their hard work, however, is the investment of the fruits of their labor. Endless, heavy labor is anything but a Chinese monopoly; millions of non-Chinese Southeast Asians are engaged in exhausting toil. The chief factor setting the Chinese apart is their ability and inclination to save for the attainment of distant goals. The willingness to make sacrifices in the present to earn returns in the future has permitted the overseas Chinese to inch their way up from poverty. Not all have succeeded, but those who have owe their rise to a propensity to save for investment. The hawker who has become a small shopkeeper, the driver who has saved to buy his own taxi, or the clerk who has studied to master the skills demanded of a manager are examples of success through sacrifice. Possibly reinforced by support from family or friends, countless individuals have advanced themselves through industry and thrift.

Just as the explanation of overseas Chinese vitality is uncertain, accounting for the inclination to save for the future can be no more than superficial. It is appropriate to suggest that the claims of the family upon members encouraged thrift. Men worked and saved not only for themselves but for their kin and their descendants. The popular notion that climate in China prompted industry may also be relevant. The succession of seasons may well have caused men to take views of longer range than those of residents of the timeless tropics. Whatever the answers may be, industry and thrift plus favorable historical circumstances to be outlined later have established the overseas Chinese in their preeminence.

Handicaps. The liabilities of the Southeast Asian Chinese have been eclipsed by their strengths. Writers have so consistently sought to dramatize the power of the overseas Chinese that the weaknesses of the people have received limited notice, but no political evaluation should attempt to walk on one leg.

Traditionally, the overseas Chinese have been reluctant to sink Southeast Asian roots. The emigrants came into the area as sojourners, men seeking their fortunes during a temporary period of exile. Few Chinese left home in the expectation that there would be no return; none ever went abroad to seek assimilation to an alien culture. The attitude of the sojourner insulated the Chinese against acculturation and raised barriers of misunderstanding between Chinese and indigenous Southeast Asians. On the one side, the overseas Chinese, excepting some early immigrants in Thailand, avoided emotional investment in their foreign homelands and sought to divorce themselves from matters of local concern. On the other side, indigenous Southeast Asians concluded that the Chinese in their midst had come only to exploit. The Chinese affected detached superiority; the local people nursed resentment.

The disdain of the sojourner for local involvement has not been restricted to the China-born. Men who have never known China at firsthand and presumably never will are nevertheless quite capable of viewing Southeast Asian residence as somehow impermanent. Racial, more properly racist, prejudices have in some instances reinforced the attitude of the sojourner. To some, isolation from the indigenous peoples is dictated not solely by cultural aloofness but also by convictions of racial superiority. In old China, race was supposedly a matter of no consequence. A man was a Chinese or a barbarian, but the determination of status was based upon cultural attainment rather than upon human type. If racial tolerance was indeed the rule, the earlier immigrants coming into Southeast Asia brought no racism with them. Racial bigotry where it exists among the overseas Chinese must have first been learned abroad. It is hard not to conclude that the lessons came from the Western colonial rulers. The original guilt may rest with those who bore the white man's burden, but some overseas Chinese became apprentices and accomplices in racism. What is worse, there are articulate, indigenous Southeast Asians who point to the existence of Chinese contempt to justify discrimination against immigrants and their descendants.

The recent independence struggles have exacerbated feelings of hostility and suspicion between the indigenous and Chinese peoples of Southeast Asia. Some nationalists charged that the Chinese were unsympathetic to their fight against colonialism. To borrow a phrase from the Communist lexicon, the Chinese were regarded as "running dogs of imperialism." Having comfortably established themselves in colonial society under Western patronage, it was believed, the Chinese sought to thwart revolution. Far more exposed than the Westerners to nationalist rage, the overseas Chinese, especially in Indonesia, were victims of violence. Fear, grief, and mistrust have yet to evaporate.

The indictment of the Chinese as servants of colonialism is not altogether baseless. As a relatively prosperous people with major investments in the area, the Chinese of Southeast Asia tended to fear destruction of the status quo by people from the depressed and despised stratum of colonial society. Often unprotected against the collapse of law and order, the Chinese suffered physical and financial injury. Those who found themselves in districts under Western military control, as did most of the urbanized settlers, had no real alternative to cooperation with the enemies of nationalist revolution. There is no consequential evidence, however, that the overseas people were ideologically wedded to colonialism. The old order, resting upon racial stratification, in some cases benefited the overseas Chinese, but it rarely seems to have won their hearts. Yet the semi-myth of counterrevolution persists.

To serve as objects of persecution a people must be visible and vulnerable. More often than not, the overseas Chinese meet both requirements. The physical distinctiveness of the Chinese appears more sharply in maritime Southeast Asia than in those countries more closely attached to China by geography and ethnology. In Malaysia, Indonesia, and the Philippines, most Chinese settlers differ recognizably in appearance from their indigenous neighbors; but even in those maritime areas, many Chinese of mixed ancestry look like the local people. In Thailand, owing to the frequency of intermarriage, and in Vietnam, because of the ancient ethnic link between the Vietnamese and the southern Chinese, the physical similarity between the local and the immigrant populations is striking. Despite these qualifications, it is true that the bulk of the overseas Chinese stand out as physically exotic in their Southeast Asian setting. In addition to their physical distinctiveness, they tend to be conspicuously urban and commercial and relatively prosperous. There can be no doubt that virtually any indigenous Southeast Asian selected at random could point out the Chinese in his village or neighborhood.

The vulnerability of the overseas Chinese results from their being in the minority wherever they reside. In Malaysia, before Singapore's secession, the Chinese formed the largest ethnic group but had been legislated into a minority position politically. For centuries, under colonialism and under independence, Chinese settlers have been pushed forward as scapegoats to cover administrative failures or to serve political ambitions. The relative wealth and the enduring insecurity of the overseas people have long fed bureaucratic corruption. In most Southeast Asian countries where extortion and persecution of the Chinese have been institutionalized, the winning of freedom from colonialism, as will be shown later, seems to have meant that mistreatment of the immigrant communities has achieved new respectability as an expression of national devotion.

The last overseas Chinese liability to consider is isolation from outside support. In the final years of the last dynasty, during the period of the Republic, and for a time after the Communist revolution, successive Chinese governments sought with irregular effect to extend diplomatic and consular protection to their citizens established abroad. Results may have been uneven, but the promise of protection comforted the overseas communities for more than half a century. Today the promise has faded. The Nationalist government on Taiwan lacks the ability to engender respect among Southeast Asian statesmen. The Chinese Communists, after initially assuming a menacing stance of guardianship over the overseas settlers, have reversed themselves. Now Peking prefers to treat the Chinese abroad as an embarrassing nuisance complicating the implementation of grand strategy. The break came at the end of the fifties when a diplomatic contest between the People's Republic of China and Indonesia brought Peking to the conclusion that cooperation from Sukarno was to be desired over gratitude from the overseas Chinese. Events since October 1965 have obliged China again to protest Indonesian mistreatment of Chinese in the country, but to date, the tone of the diplomatic notes has been more routine than ominous.

A brief preliminary catalogue of the more typical disabilities encountered in the recent past by the Chinese of Southeast Asia may lend perspective to this examination. Official treatment of the Chinese minorities ranges from blatant discrimination in Indonesia to the relative liberality of Malaysia. In no country are the Chinese crushed, nor is there any place other than their own Singapore where they enjoy maximum freedom and security. The major matters in which the Chinese are pressed are citizenship, economic opportunity, education, and language. Only to the extent that conversion to Christianity facilitates naturalization in the Philippines or that acceptance of Islam might bring benefits in Muslim strongholds is there any religious challenge to the Chinese of the region.

At different times and places, the issue of citizenship for people of Chinese origin has overshadowed the other concerns of the settlers. Makers of policy in Southeast Asia have long wrestled with the problem. Some have concluded, as did the government of South Vietnam in 1956, that the imposition of citizenship on all locally-born Chinese would break down communalism and generate a new loyalty. Others believe that the Chinese should not be permitted to acquire easily the protective cloak of local citizenship. That second line of reasoning has led to the erection of hurdles on the path to naturalization in the Philippines and, on a lesser scale, in Malaysia, Brunei, and Thailand. There would seem to be no generally applicable answer to the question. The Chinese of South Vietnam appeared to feel that the Saigon government opened its arms in preparation for squeezing. In Malaysia, Thailand, and the Philippines, some overseas Chinese assert that citizenship is held back in order to maintain their vulnerability to discrimination. Jakarta and Peking have both used the citizenship tangle in their diplomatic exchanges. The story of the negotiations leading to the implementation of the Sino-Indonesian treaty on citizenship is lengthy and does not require retelling here. There are, however, two points to bear in mind when one considers this feature of the travails of the Chinese in Indonesia. First, the only mass political movement of that people, known as Baperki, was founded to aid in the struggle for local citizenship. Although Baperki has branched out to concern itself with the education, culture, and politics of the Chinese, its central purpose remains the clarification of the issue of nationality and of the rights of citizens. Second, Sukarno's government has made such effective use of a formula distinguishing citizens of alien ancestry from those of indigenous roots that naturalization brings but limited benefits.

Steps to contain the economic dynamism of Chinese settlers have been taken in all the countries of the region. The objectives of such efforts are to safeguard traditional rights and open up new opportunities for indigenous peoples. The theory, unflattering though it might at first seem, is that without special protection those of local ancestry cannot compete with the Chinese.

In colonial times, it was generally customary for the Chinese to be denied the right to own and farm land. Entry into military or bureaucratic service was similarly all but impossible. The colonial authorities seemed to have had mixed motives. By shielding the local peasantry from Chinese pressure, they thought a humanitarian goal was served. Reserving most lower- and middle-range government posts for indigenous clerks and soldiers was likewise considered benevolent. Occupational segregation, however, was also a cornerstone of rule through division. During the colonial centuries, the Chinese were by and large content. There was work for them to do, and their own economic roles were secure.

With the winning of independence, the old pluralism came under attack. The leaders of the emerging sovereign states universally endorsed the belief that Chinese occupational monopolies were unjust. In particular, they felt that indigenous participation in the non-agricultural sectors of the economy ought to be increased. It hardly needs to be added that there was no corresponding conviction that the Chinese deserved access to farming and state employment.

Economic nationalism in Southeast Asia has been expressed in a variety of ways. In Thailand and in South Vietnam, lists of occupations open only to citizens have been published officially. The Philippine government has legislated out of existence the small Chinese-owned retail shop. Indonesian authorities have sought to exclude the Chinese from retail trade in rural areas. In some cases, these restrictions can be avoided by those Chinese in possession of local citizenship; in others, it has become necessary to work through indigenous fronts.

In Indonesia and in Malaysia, citizenship does not preclude official discrimination. The Jakarta government has been frankly discriminatory in the granting of licenses to operate certain businesses—most notably in the import-export trade. Once again, the front man comes into his own. In Malaysia, the "sons of the soil" (including many first- or second-generation "Malays" of Indonesian ancestry), in contrast to men of Chinese or Indian origin, receive preferential treatment in the allocation of business licenses, such as those required to open highway transport firms. Posts in the civil service of Malaya are supposed to be filled by four Malays for every non-Malay, Chinese, or Indian, although the quota system has been unevenly effective and is applied in a variety of ways at the different levels of the bureaucracy.

As the argument to be developed in this study will favor the assimilation of the Chinese into the general societies of the Southeast Asian countries, there can be no quarrel with the idea of breaking down economic exclusivism. There is room, however, for the belief that care should be exercised lest economic nationalism merely stir Chinese resentment and impede economic growth. Ideally, the Chinese middle class should be supplemented, not destroyed. With customary clarity, C. P. Fitzgerald sums it up:

Free enterprise must mean that capitalists are given scope to carry out their operations, restrained from too great an exploitation of the workers, but unhampered by racist ideologies and excessive nationalist policies. In South East Asia the capitalists are the Chinese. It is not possible to discriminate against capitalists because they are Chinese and at the same time successfully oppose communism, because that, too, is backed by China. In the long run South East Asian countries must decide whether they want Chinese capitalism or Chinese communism, and the run is not going to be very long.[1]

The picture in Burma is somewhat different because economic nationalism has been most militantly directed against the Indian community, historically the dominant alien middle class. Furthermore, current attacks on Chinese business interests are part of the general effort to progress along the "Burmese Way to

[1] C. P. Fitzgerald, "Overseas Chinese in South East Asia," *The Australian Journal of Politics and History*, v. 8, no. 1, May 1962, p. 77.

Socialism." The nationalization of retail shops, for example, is not anti-Chinese per se, though of course the consequences for the victims of expropriation are the same. In one sense, however, the situation in Burma can be considered uniquely hostile to Chinese enterprise, for there is not even the chance to operate through indigenous fronts.

Chinese education in this century has provided a foundation for nationalism and has been the main theater of community endeavor. Chinese schooling has also served to isolate many overseas Chinese from their indigenous neighbors. Glorious though Chinese learning may be, cultural chauvinism is a high price to pay for refinement in a foreign tradition. As a general feature of programs to shake the settlers loose from their attachment to China, Southeast Asian governments have sought to nationalize, at least in part, the schooling of Chinese children. Official restrictions run from informal censorship of textbooks to the padlocking of schools. In between are schemes obliging children to master the local language, selective subsidization of Chinese schools, and limitations on the number of years a pupil may follow a Chinese curriculum. So decisive have been these measures that outside of the Borneo territories of Malaysia, fewer than half the overseas Chinese children attend Chinese schools.[2] Later, particular attention will be paid to the nature of this phenomenon in Singapore; here it needs merely to be pointed out that unlike all the other cases, official encouragement has not been a decisive factor in the rising popularity of non-Chinese education in Singapore.

No doubt in large part because anti-Sinicism has been inconspicuous in Burma, Chinese schools in that country have not felt the weight of official hostility. It is reported that Chinese education is losing community support in Burma, but the explanation would seem to be in factors other than meddling by the government.

Moving eastward, one sees that the Thai government is nearing completion of the work of a quarter of a century to break the back of Chinese education. It is anticipated that Chinese children

[2] Douglas P. Murray, "Chinese Education in South East Asia," *The China Quarterly*, no. 20, October/December 1964, p. 71. Much of the material presented here is expanded upon in this highly useful article.

in the country will soon be obliged to have three years of non-Chinese schooling if they elect to receive the maximum four years of Chinese primary education now permitted. Because of the complexities of learning written Chinese, Bangkok will thus have made it all but impossible for Chinese children to master their ancestral tongue. Private tutors may instruct some children, but as older generations die off, there will be fewer and fewer people in Thailand capable of reading a Chinese newspaper or of understanding the Chinese national language. The process of assimilation now well begun will receive new impetus.

In Malaysia, Chinese education has been losing ground. The governments in the former federation all considered plans to limit the Chinese content of curricula, although Singapore and the Borneo states moved slowly. The schools on the peninsula probably reveal the shape of things to come. Through its financial power over private institutions receiving state aid, the government in Kuala Lumpur has engineered the replacement of Chinese with English or Malay as the chief medium of instruction at the secondary level. This scheme will make it difficult for a child to go beyond primary school unless he has mastery over a non-Chinese language. Consequently Chinese primary education, although not directly under attack, is destined to fall behind. Finally, the most forceful evidence that Kuala Lumpur inclines to be unfriendly to Chinese education was seen in the refusal of the Malaysian government to grant aid to the Chinese university at Singapore, Nanyang, or to recognize the degrees of its graduates.

As it has done in so many other areas of overseas Chinese life, the Indonesian government has struck heavy blows on the Chinese educational system. Only alien Chinese children are permitted to go to schools partially Chinese in curriculum, but even in those institutions, Indonesian language and history are required subjects. Citizens are obliged to attend national schools where the training is thoroughly Indonesian. The mass organization of the Indonesian citizen Chinese, Baperki, has been active in setting up schools where, despite curricular nationalization, student bodies are heavily Chinese in ancestry. De facto segregation of Chinese from indigenous children thus survives. Seeking higher education, the Chinese youth of Indonesia must either be qualified to matriculate in an Indonesian-language institution or go abroad.

South Vietnamese authorities have not sought to close Chinese schools, but stringent regulation of these institutions has been imposed. The government has been unable so far to realize its aims of tolerating only Vietnamese citizens as principals and of making faculties predominantly Vietnamese in nationality; however, the use of Chinese as the primary language of instruction has been prohibited. Children now study Chinese as they might an alien tongue. In Laos, the small Chinese community has been most concerned with whether its schools would be oriented toward Peking or Taipei, while in Cambodia, that question has been resolved by Prince Sihanouk's amicable relations with the People's Republic.

Finally, with respect to education, it can be observed that Manila has been quite tolerant of Chinese schooling. This fact is due both to diplomatic friendship with Taipei and, presumably, to the willingness of the Philippine authorities to see a continuation of Chinese separatism as a means of retarding assimilation, which would enable more Chinese to escape official scrutiny and pressure. Fear that Chinese schools might, despite their link with the Nationalist embassy, become centers for Communist indoctrination may bring about a change in Manila's stand of *laissez faire*.

Language is the last area of discrimination to consider. Only in Singapore is Chinese fully recognized as an official language, and even there, Malay is equally favored. Governments elsewhere either grudgingly tolerate the survival of the language or work out a scheme for its suppression. In South Vietnam and in Thailand, for example, shop signs may not be exclusively in Chinese characters. In the Philippines, firms are not allowed to keep books solely in Chinese. Although the prohibition has recently been rescinded, the Indonesian government for some years outlawed the printing of newspapers in Chinese. As the restrictions on Chinese education expand and take hold, the need for such curbs on the use of the Chinese language will fade.

All the factors listed above and their interrelation will be treated further. At this point, it is only necessary to re-emphasize the diversity of the Chinese in Southeast Asia and to list again their assets of education, information, industry, and thrift, and their handicaps of rootlessness, intolerance, vulnerability, and isolation. The current state of overseas Chinese society will be examined in more detail later; first, it is sensible to prepare by taking a look at history.

CHAPTER THREE

Historical Foundations

Links between China and the lands to her south were established in distant antiquity. As Chinese culture spread in the last millennium before Christ from its birthplace on the banks of the Yellow River, it encountered cultures ancestral to those of some modern Southeast Asians. The Thai, Lao, and Vietnamese peoples, for example, all have remote roots in regions long politically Chinese. As the frontier of Chinese settlement was advanced, enclaves of peoples destined to become ethnic minorities, in the manner of American Indians, were bypassed. Other peoples in southern and western China were absorbed by the Chinese in a process which continues, reportedly at an accelerated pace, today.

Below the line of Chinese settlement, Southeast Asian societies have grown. Since imperial unification by the Ch'in dynasty in the third century B.C., the cultural and political lines of demarcation between China and Southeast Asia have been sharpened. Only in Vietnam did Chinese influence achieve paramountcy through Chinese colonial rule for more than ten centuries. Although freedom from Chinese political control was won by the Vietnamese a thousand years ago in what can presumably be called Southeast Asia's first independence struggle, Chinese cultural supremacy survived. Southeast Asia was historically divided into three spheres: Vietnam, where Chinese culture dominated; the arc of lands running southeast from Burma through Indonesia, where Indian currents were powerful; and the relatively remote Philippines, where weaker influences from both China and India were felt. Islam became a strong tide in the region about five hundred years ago and spread principally to the maritime lands, Malaysia, Indonesia, and the southern Philippines.

Early Chinese Ties with Southeast Asia

During the more than twenty centuries so hastily surveyed, Chinese ties with Southeast Asia, at first tenuous but later substantial, were formed. Dynastic records speak of diplomatic and commercial exchange developed almost from the beginning of China's long imperial history. Tribute missions from Southeast Asia were frequent bearers of respect for the Chinese emperor and exotic goods for the Chinese market. Archaeological finds in Southeast Asia reveal that Chinese ceramics were shipped south from an early date. Few Chinese traders seem to have reached those areas of Southeast Asia accessible only by sea in the first centuries of contact, but improvements in shipbuilding and navigation ultimately were to make China a great maritime power in the region. By the end of the thirteenth century, the Mongol emperor of China was able to dispatch an armada to the Indonesian archipelago. Although the invasion was a failure, it is supposed to have left behind deserters or stragglers who may have become the first permanent Chinese settlers in the area. During the first third of the fifteenth century, the Ming dynasty sponsored a series of great naval expeditions to Southeast Asia and far beyond. Unlike its Iberian counterparts in the same century, the Chinese court, not driven by crusading zeal, international rivalry, and fiscal hunger to build an empire upon maritime foundations, abandoned exploration; but a private Chinese commercial empire was already taking shape overseas. When the first Portuguese came to Southeast Asia in the beginning of the sixteenth century, Chinese traders were there to greet them.

From the opening of the era of Western colonialism with the Portuguese capture of Malacca in 1511, the Chinese in the region sought to accommodate themselves to the changing order in Southeast Asia. Sometimes tolerated, on occasion savagely attacked, the overseas Chinese learned to live under Western rule.

The operation of licensed monopolies under the East India companies of the British and the Dutch was profitable to many; private commerce gave livelihoods to others. For three and a half centuries, the Chinese population of the region grew at a moderate pace; there were simply not enough opportunities in a slowly developing economy to attract multitudes of immigrants.

The Flood Tide of Chinese Immigration, 1860–1930

About the middle of the nineteenth century, Southeast Asia entered a period of quickened transformation. The decline of mercantilism had heralded the death of Dutch and British company rule; conditions hospitable to free trade appeared. Corresponding with the opening of greatly expanded opportunities for private investment was a growing demand for Southeast Asian products to feed Western industrialization. The whole process of development was speeded by the opening of the Suez Canal in 1869, possibly the most significant date in Southeast Asian economic history. Tin, tobacco, and, later, rubber production doubled and redoubled. So rapid was economic expansion that chronic labor shortages appeared. Indigenous peasants, by and large, were reluctant to leave their villages to work under the disciplined and often harsh conditions of large-scale mining and estate agriculture. Labor had to be recruited outside the region. India sent immigrants, but China sent vastly greater numbers.

The story of the first great waves of nineteenth-century Chinese emigration is horrifying. A brief description of the operation of what was known as the coolie trade seems in order. Typically, villagers were recruited by agents, known as coolie crimps. Sometimes false promises lured men to sign away their freedom; other men in effect sold themselves to pay off their debts. The recruits were assembled in ports and lodged in barracoons. (That this old term for the pens used on the African coast to confine slaves was transplanted to China is in itself revealing.) Packed aboard vessels, the coolies sailed for new lands. Many, of course, died on the voyage; coolie mutinies were the terror of the crews. Upon arrival, say at Singapore, the semi-slaves were normally kept on board their ships until brokers, serving either Chinese or European enterprises, contracted for their labor in a process colloquially referred to by the Chinese as "buying pigs." The healthy and the skilled commanded the highest prices; the sickly were unwanted. Once ashore, the men worked out the years of their contracts; and if they made the grade and lived, they became free settlers or sought to return home.

The voyage south from China grew smoother as the nineteenth century advanced. Square-rigged vessels took the place of junks and were in turn replaced by steamships. The blossoming of Victorian humanitarianism and the awakening in the Peking court of mandarin concern for emigrant sons ultimately brought an end to the coolie traffic. Migration and settlement abroad no longer meant humiliation and hazard.

The millions of Chinese who arrived during the flood tide of immigration from about 1860 to 1930 almost all shared three characteristics. Without meaningful exception, all were poor; and until around the start of our current century, only a fragment were women. There is nothing unique in these points. Economic distress has historically and universally been the prime cause of emigration; and immigrant and frontier communities, whether in Australia, California, or Sumatra, typically have been heavily male in composition. The third general characteristic of the Chinese immigrants did set them apart from most other men who have left home for newer lands. The Chinese looked homeward with enduring nostalgia. China was more than the old country. It was the only country worthy of respect and capable of being understood. The rest of the world was worse than alien. It was incomprehensible. Success abroad could be measured by the strength of a man's ties to China. Sending money back to relatives in the old village was an obligation borne seemingly by all but the destitute. Prosperity permitted a man to bring a wife from China. Wealthy men bought Chinese household furnishings, built tasteless approximations of the houses of the elite back home, and engaged tutors to come south to teach their children. Ideally, hard work and thrift abroad were rewarded by retirement and repatriation or, less ideally, by shipment north for burial. As has already been noted, there may have been men who sailed from China expecting never to return, but there was none who cheerfully hoped for permanent expatriation. The contrast with emigrants leaving Europe for America is striking and significant. This attitude of sojourner or transient was to become a handicap for Chinese abroad.

Uprooted immigrant hordes could not be controlled by the thin ranks of the colonial bureaucracies. In those areas where new settlers were most numerous, arrangements for their indirect rule were developed through both official design and immigrant ingenuity. The colonial administrations of earlier periods had hit upon schemes for the supervision of the Chinese through the medium of various headmen, often assigned quasi-military titles. The Captain China in places such as Malacca and Batavia was selected on the basis of his wealth and power. In return for the prestige and perquisites of his office, the Captain was expected to serve as the intermediary between the Europeans and the Chinese. The system worked so long as the Chinese communities were fairly stable in size and placid in conduct. Before the huge influx of immigrants, the Chinese quarters of the cities and towns were generally not trouble spots. The Europeans and the Chinese normally complemented one another in their economic endeavors; both groups appeared content with the system of headmen.

The immigrant flood shattered the old serenity. The numbers of rootless, restless men were too great to fit into a pattern of administration resting upon the headman's control through business connections, kinship, and patronage. The enormously expanded Chinese populations, especially in mining and estate areas of rapid development, had to shift for themselves in improvising a political order of sorts. The tradition of the secret society provided the techniques required.

Secret societies have deep roots in Chinese history. Starting as heretical expressions, the societies inevitably assumed a politically subversive character, for in imperial China the charismatic emperor enjoyed divine ordination. To challenge any part of the harmonious order was to threaten the whole. The clandestine brotherhoods imported into Southeast Asia displayed the religious orientation of their forerunners, and they voiced rebelliousness in the slogan: "Overthrow the Manchus, restore the Ming." In their overseas location, however, disobedience to the dynasty was long largely a matter of form. There was immediate work to be done.

In effect, the secret societies had to give protection and order to the immigrants. Membership brought a man into a circle of brothers who could assist in the process of survival abroad. Companionship, employment, relief, and defense were all supposed to be had within the order. The brotherhoods thus sought to substitute for families left in China. Acknowledging no law but their own, the secret societies turned to crime; but lawlessness was not their fundamental purpose. The profits of crime were in the nature of revenues for the underground governments of the immigrants. As other forms of organization gained strength in the nineteenth century, the secret societies lost vitality and prestige. Today the brotherhoods have deteriorated into gangster mobs; but for a time, a century or so ago, the societies played a positive role in the resettlement of green immigrants.

Operating in the open were other kinds of organizations to serve the settlers. The so-called territorial associations recruited members on the basis of place of origin or language. Kinship associations served those sharing the same surnames and thus claiming descent from common ancestors. The blood tie might be more imagined than real, but the feeling of kinship among members was likely to be genuine enough. Trade and craft associations, later joined by chambers of commerce and labor unions, brought together men of like occupations and economic aims. All these open organizations were actively supported. Indeed, one might belong to several as well as to a secret society. As the administrations of Southeast Asia sought means of supervising and communicating with the Chinese, the open associations often received semi-official recognition. The chambers of commerce in particular tended to be regarded as agencies to transmit Chinese desires to the government and to broadcast and interpret official policies to the Chinese communities. The imperial and republican governments of China used the chambers of commerce similarly.

During the nineteenth and twentieth centuries the Chinese increased not only in numbers but in economic power. The process leading to Chinese domination of the bulk of Southeast Asia's commerce presumably began at some unknown date far back in history when the first Chinese immigrant trader opened for business. The development from the time of mass immigration was thus new in degree, not in kind. From about the middle of the previous century, Chinese moved toward economic mastery with greater speed and in larger numbers than ever before. As Western capital stimulated the production of primary products for export, there was more for the Chinese intermediary trader to do. As relative prosperity came to some areas, there were more customers for the Chinese retailer. As pacification and direct administration of hinterlands progressed, the Chinese merchants ranged farther afield. There remains, however, the perplexing question of why the Chinese rather than some other peoples saw and seized the new economic opportunities.

Except in Burma, where the Indians enjoyed ascendancy in business, and in Cambodia and remote Laos, where the Vietnamese approached similar success, the Chinese were little challenged in their economic rise. Industry and thrift have already been pointed out as priceless, if hard to explain, Chinese gifts. Organizational ability and communications systems also served the Chinese settlers. Furthermore, it is true that the immigrants reached the right place at the right time.

The very fact of immigration was perhaps most decisive. Torn away from traditional pursuits and ancient restraints, the overseas settlers could move into activities rarely accessible to their kinfolk in the home villages. Heavily peasant in background, the immigrants normally did not seek to farm in Southeast Asia. Laws against land alienation, the scarcity of capital for investment in farmsteads, and the near absence of wives and children to help work family farms all were obstacles to the establishment of Chinese peasants in the region. More important, it seems, was the fact that Chinese migration was more than an international transplanting of people. It was in the pattern of movement from the farms to the cities that has been a feature of all modern economic growth. The Chinese left not only their country but the countryside as well. Working as miners or estate laborers for a time after reaching the tropics, most overseas Chinese gravitated toward urban areas and city occupations. The indigenous peoples living within social structures of only two levels, peasant and noble, for the most part remained rooted to their traditions and were unprepared for economic adventure.

Engaged in occupations alien to the indigenous peasants, performing tasks beneath the Westerners and the Southeast Asian nobility, the Chinese occupied the middle rung on the economic ladder. Thousands of them worked at light-industrial and service jobs, but vastly more vital were those involved in trade. Local goods were bought up from village producers, transported, processed, and sold to exporters by Chinese roaming the back country. Imported manufactures reached consumers, frequently on credit, through Chinese channels leading from port warehouses to retail shops and itinerant peddlers. Correspondingly, the internal commerce of most countries was largely in Chinese hands. The great Western trading firms could not have reached the masses of indigenous producers and consumers without Chinese intermediaries, nor could the flow of local goods between rural and urban areas have attained much volume in their absence. Virtually no transaction was too petty for the immigrant traders; and, as time went on, few endeavors were too large to be attempted by Chinese management and capital. It was inadequate to say, as did a much-worn cliché, that the Westerners held the Southeast Asian cow while the Chinese merely milked her. Before it could be milked, the cow had to be caught and brought in from pasture, and these tasks were Chinese too.

Near the end of the nineteenth century, there began an overseas Chinese political awakening that has continued through decades of change to the present. The start of the process is usually referred to as a birth of nationalism among the Chinese abroad. The reasons for the shift in attitude from a comparatively passive sentimental attachment to the land and culture of China to a dynamic, on occasion aggressive, identification with the Chinese nation are many and complex. It is appropriate here simply to record the fact that for nearly seventy years the Chinese abroad, like their compatriots at home, have been caught up in the nationalist tide of our era. China came to be viewed not merely with cultural homesickness; the Chinese nation, including its overseas members, was believed to be the entity through which individual and collective hopes were to be realized. Threats to the nation endangered every Chinese; national triumphs rewarded all.

Recognition of the Chinese as a nation struggling among other nations rather than as the sole civilized people in a global sea of barbarism came swiftly. The change was first prompted by those dynastic officials who sought to revitalize China. The dispatch of imperial missions to foreign lands and the establishment of consulates and legations abroad generated an awareness in Peking of overseas Chinese problems and strengths. The revenue-producing potential of the settlers abroad was especially impressive to the Manchu court. Close on the heels of the mandarins came conservative reformers to enlist the overseas people in the cause of national salvation through modernization. Shortly, the revolutionaries under Sun Yat-sen appeared and assumed leadership.

Lip service to the cause of Manchu overthrow had consistently been paid by the secret societies, so the revolutionary message promising a Chinese restoration had a familiar ring in Southeast Asia. Furthermore, as overseas Chinese nationalism was ardently directed toward pulling China out of her backwardness, Sun Yat-sen's vaguely phrased program for social and economic advance appealed to the Chinese abroad. Uncounted sums of overseas Chinese money went into the revolutionary treasury; cells of the revolutionary party were founded throughout Southeast Asia. It would not be fanciful to argue that without the support of the Chinese abroad, the destruction of the dynasty would have been achieved later and possibly under different auspices. The 1911 revolution, much unlike that of 1949, was in considerable measure an expression of the nationalism of the overseas Chinese. The party of Sun Yat-sen, renamed the Kuomintang, was to be the focus of overseas Chinese national loyalty until after World War II.

Two twentieth-century developments, one the product of the other, were instrumental in the emergence of revolutionary nationalism among the overseas Chinese. The modernized school system, dating from the beginning of the century, and the growing use of Mandarin as an immigrant *lingua franca* have been the cradle and vehicle of nationalism. The traditional schools had been inadequate in terms of education and political indoctrination; their successors have displayed strength in both areas. Nothing has been more central to the nationalist mobilization of the overseas Chinese than the political recruitment conducted in the classrooms. Boycotts, demonstrations, even violence have originated in the schools; and the language of overseas Chinese nationalism has been the Mandarin learned there. The Chinese have been most forceful politically in those places in Southeast Asia, such as Malaysia, where their schools have flourished. The intensity of their nationalism, like the quality of their Mandarin, has been lower where Chinese education was held back.

The 1930s and Early 1940s

The Kuomintang as the leader of wartime China rose to a zenith of influence and prestige among the overseas Chinese in the 1930s and early 1940s. The two external dangers to their nation, Western imperialism and Japanese aggression, stirred the Chinese to resistance. Thirty years after the fact, Chinese resentment toward the West may seem secondary in importance. But at the time, most of the unequal treaty system was still in force in China; and old-style imperialism was in vigorous old age. The presence of foreign concessions, alien gunboats, extraterritorial courts, and the rest of the symbols and realities of China's humiliation proved that national independence was not yet won. Past and rightly anticipated military attacks by the Japanese caused fear for the survival of the Chinese nation. Since most Chinese in Southeast Asia had direct and daily contact with Western colonial rule, semi-colonialism in the ancestral land was particularly offensive. As expatriates hoping to obtain dignity and protection from a reborn China, the overseas people were especially alarmed by the Japanese menace. Men looked to the Kuomintang to rescue the nation through combat with imperialism and defense against Japan.

For some overseas Chinese, intense hostility toward imperialism and alarm over Japanese expansion led to receptiveness to communism. The line between the far left of the Kuomintang and the

Communists in Southeast Asia, as in China, was blurred. Sun Yat-sen's economic and political doctrines were sufficiently fuzzy in formulation to permit arbitrary, indeed opportunistic, interpretation. The recruitment of Communist cadres among the virulently nationalistic overseas Chinese youth, especially in Singapore and Malaya, progressed; and there were efforts to use the developing strength of the labor movement for Communist ends. The testing of the Communists and all other overseas Chinese was soon to come under the Japanese occupation.

Japan's conquest and rule of Southeast Asia struck cruel blows against the Chinese. The colonial order under which the immigrants had advanced and the world trade upon which they ultimately depended for their livelihoods were destroyed. No longer could Chinese rely on their knowledge of administrative ways and on their central role in the colonial system to win security; nor could they hope to prosper from the direct and the indirect profits of international exchange. Wartime isolation stagnated the economies of the region. The Japanese military administration was inept, and, worse, its actions were unpredictable. Men could survive only through black marketeering, speculation, or subsistence agriculture.

Bad government and economic deterioration were not the only disasters to afflict the overseas Chinese during the war. The Japanese singled out the Chinese settlers for markedly harsh treatment. In their fervor of triumph in the first days of the occupation, the Japanese massacred thousands. The extent of the conquerors' savagery will never be precisely known. Not long ago, for example, old fears were confirmed by the discovery in Singapore of a mass grave of Chinese victims. As the excitement of combat was replaced by the tedium of occupation duty, Japanese forces became more selective in their terror. Chinese community leaders were ordered to raise lavish gifts of money, nominally for the emperor, to express gratitude for the new order in Southeast Asia. Persons suspected of underground resistance were rounded up, tortured, and murdered. Chinese guerrilla bands, like their Filipino allies, were pursued and fought. The occupation brought suffering to all and death to many. Overseas Chinese collaboration with the Japanese was generally uncommon because the settlers were for the most part committed to the cause of Chinese national salvation and because the Japanese had little need for and less faith in Chinese traitors. Efforts to harness the power of Southeast Asian nationalism for Japanese purposes through propaganda demanding "Asia for the Asiatics" led to the creation of indigenous administrative and military organizations. Perhaps more Chinese collaborationists would have appeared had the policies of the Japanese occupation not favored the enlistment of indigenous puppets, but the fact remains that for most overseas Chinese, the road to treachery was closed.

Japanese mistrust of the overseas Chinese was far from groundless. The settlers had contributed enormous sums to the Chinese war chest as it was moved in retreat from Nanking to Hankow and finally to Chungking. No other Chinese population was more dedicated to national defense; Chiang Kai-shek commanded no more loyal followers. Until late in the war, the Chinese and the Filipinos were the only peoples in Southeast Asia to offer major resistance to the Japanese. In Malaya, where the proportion and nationalism of the Chinese were greatest, the fight against Japan began as the invaders moved down the peninsula and continued throughout the years of occupation. Distressing though it may be retrospectively, the most effective guerrillas were organized and led by a tightly knit Chinese Communist minority of a few thousand. Veterans of that force were to return to the jungle in 1948 to become terrorists in a campaign to dislodge the colonial and, after 1957, the Malayan authorities. Except for contained remnants, the Chinese Communist guerrillas had been defeated by 1953, although the war, euphemistically designated the Emergency, was not officially declared ended until 1960.

The ability of the Communists in Malaya to mobilize military threats for nearly two decades is a measure of their resourcefulness and discipline rather than of their numbers. Presumably prewar years of clandestine operation had equipped the Communists with the communications and intelligence techniques needed to support guerrilla forces. Funds and supplies were obtained, in part through intimidation, from urban Chinese. Food, local intelligence, and sometimes shelter were available from Chinese peasants on the edges of the jungle. The economic decay of the occupation period had driven many to subsistence farming on unclaimed or unposted land away from urban centers. Such men were known as squatters because of their unlawful occupancy of their farms. The squatters were invaluable to the Communists during the war against Japan and during the Emergency. The chief positive effort of the British and Malayan authorities in the defeat of the terrorists took the form of relocating the squatters to deny food and information to the guerrillas.

The Postwar Years

Victory over Japan brought new uncertainties to the overseas Chinese. The revolutionary bursting of Southeast Asian nationalism, touched off by the war, endangered many and dictated readjustment for all. Antipathy toward the Chinese in their midst had long smoldered among many indigenous Southeast Asians. Colonial administrators had been largely content and relieved in the prewar plural societies to have Chinese settlers serve as immediate targets of native vexation. The Japanese, bringing to the region their own fierce hostility toward the Chinese and their program to win indigenous backing for the "greater East Asia coprosperity sphere," consciously exacerbated intercommunal ill will. Strife between the Chinese and their neighbors was never more ghastly than in the time of anarchy between the Japanese collapse and the re-establishment of law enforcement. In Malaya and Indonesia, the Chinese suffered most acutely.

The nationalist revolutionaries of postwar Southeast Asia called for both liberation from colonialism and economic advance, while they held the Chinese to be agents of Western exploitation and obstacles to material progress. Vengeance against the Chinese was most brutal in Indonesia, where the process of revolution was violent and lengthy. Slaughters of rural Chinese frightened survivors into hasty urban resettlement. In the Philippines and in Malaya, where independence came peacefully, and in the Indochinese states, where the immigrants tended to be concentrated in a few, relatively secure places, little Chinese blood was spilled. In all the colonies, however, it was popularly expected that the end of Western rule would loosen the commercial grasp of the Chinese. As has been shown, indigenous economic nationalism in some form plays a role in all the political programs of independent Southeast Asia; and throughout the entire region, the Chinese experience disabilities ranging from legislated discrimination, usually in transparent disguise, to peremptory confiscation of property and denial of opportunity.

Moreover, less direct attacks on the Chinese economic position were implicit in the revolutionary remolding of Southeast Asia. The plural structure of society, most sharply seen in the form of the prewar economic ladder of three rungs—in ascending order, native, Chinese, and Western—was shaken with the winning of independence. The Western business elite was no longer automatically favored by protection from compatriots serving as administrative allies. The independent governments uniformly sought to promote indigenous entrepreneurship. These efforts ranged from mild programs such as "Malayanization" or "Malaysianization," which generated government pressure for the substitution of local for Western personnel, to the seizure of foreign property, as in Indonesia. For the middle-class Chinese, all schemes to foster indigenous upward mobility dictated the establishment of ties with a changing elite. The commercial structure resting on relationships between firms and between individuals, particularly credit relationships, was recast. The dispossession, accomplished or promised, of the Westerners opened broader avenues for some Chinese capital. To the bulk of the Chinese business community, however, perplexity rather than opportunity developed. The commerce of Southeast Asia remains largely in Chinese hands, but caution and confusion have become common moods among Chinese traders. In this as in all other areas of overseas Chinese life, there are differences among the countries of the region.

The march of history has thus quickened in cadence for the overseas Chinese. More and more change has been compressed into each succeeding decade of the twentieth century, and the present decade will likely prove to be the most challenging yet. The overseas Chinese at least have the advantage of long experience in meeting adversity and in mastering the unprecedented.

CHAPTER FOUR

The Maneuvers
of the Communists
and the Nationalists

Difficult though it may be to attempt to assess with accuracy the
political loyalties of the Chinese in Southeast Asia, some useful
insights can be gained by study of the techniques and manner of
the rival appeals from Taipei and Peking. It is surely not unreasonable to assume that both the Nationalists and the Communists seek
to project images of themselves which will win positive responses
among the Chinese abroad. After more than fifteen years of experi-
mentation, the directors of both Chinese propaganda efforts presumably have learned how best to employ their talents and resources. If it can be determined that they have consistently favored
a particular propaganda emphasis, the conclusion that the tactic
was deemed promising or necessary is not unreasonable. Thus, it is
appropriate to begin measuring the relative positions of the Nationalists and the Communists by taking inventory of the propaganda wares the two offer the overseas Chinese. Such a starting
point permits some understanding of the overseas Chinese perspective on the politics of China.

The Nationalist Effort

The Nationalist effort has followed a steadier course than that
of the Communists and is therefore more easily discussed. Denied

51

a central role in global power politics and unencumbered by revolutionary strategy, the government in Taipei, unlike that at Peking, has not been obliged to shape and reshape its interest in the overseas Chinese to meet international exigencies and the demands of dogma. It is reported that policy toward the Chinese abroad has figured in factional differences within the political hierarchy in Taipei, but the fundamental concerns of the Nationalists have been to keep their following or at least to minimize losses. The Communists, in contrast, have had to work toward the normally irreconcilable goals of enlisting overseas Chinese support and of manipulating indigenous Southeast Asian nationalism and its leaders.

The Nationalists carried to their Taiwan retreat a tradition of concern for the Chinese abroad. Quite properly, since the Revolution of 1911, no major Kuomintang statement of purposes and principles has ignored the overseas Chinese. Emigrants had sustained Sun Yat-sen in his years of exile and had made decisive sacrifices to achieve dynastic overthrow. Sun Yat-sen and his political heirs never forgot their debt to the Chinese abroad for support in the Revolution and for loyalty and generosity in meeting the later Japanese attack on China. (Parenthetically, yet appropriately, it should be noted that the Communists owe the overseas Chinese nothing. Mao Tse-tung's revolution was not nurtured by expatriates. Peking's current willingness to neglect most of the Chinese abroad may in part be explained by this historical circumstance, but there are other, weightier reasons which will be examined later.)

It has been no more than natural for the Nationalists to work to retain their overseas following. Until the Communist conquest of the China mainland, the Kuomintang had enjoyed all but unanimous backing among politically conscious Chinese abroad. Thus in 1949, the Taipei government had merely to prevent defection among the overseas Chinese. The task was straightforward, though far from easy. By definition, political and propaganda programs which seek to preserve are conservative; and, as with military rear guards, losses are irreplaceable. As counterrevolutionaries, the Nationalists could not be oriented toward revolution, although the Southeast Asian Chinese have something of a rebellious tradition and live in a revolutionary environment. In part because of the dilemma of the Kuomintang, its strength abroad has been relentlessly eroded, although it must quickly be added that deserters did not necessarily join Communist ranks.

Nationalist losses in Southeast Asia are both painful and alarming to the leaders in Taipei. More vital than the sentimental tie between the party of Sun Yat-sen and the overseas Chinese is the fact that backing from Chinese communities abroad nourishes the Nationalists in their resolute opposition to communism and their enduring hope for a return to the mainland. A simple comparison of the sizes of the overseas and the Taiwan populations demonstrates that more than half the Chinese with whom the Kuomintang can hope to keep in contact are overseas Chinese. If the Nationalists were denied all hope of overseas sympathy, exile on Taiwan would become far more forlorn. The Nationalists need the overseas people and give them much attention; the Communists can regard the loyalty of settlers abroad as a useful prize rather than as a foundation for survival. After all, Peking is not obliged to seek overseas support merely to rally a few million more Chinese to its flag. The overseas Chinese as instruments, real or potential, of Communist policy interest Peking, but to a government ruling seven hundred millions, the settlers' numbers mean little.

Taipei is also guided in its campaign toward the Chinese abroad by considerations of international prestige and diplomatic status. In those countries where the Nationalists are recognized diplomatically and can thus seek to serve as legitimate spokesmen and mediators for the overseas Chinese, their claim to be the government of China is bolstered. The efforts of Taipei to maintain its status through diplomacy are well known. In the United Nations and through the costly maintenance of embassies in dozens of capitals, the Nationalist government strives to justify its survival. Where the overseas Chinese are assumed to be responsive to Nationalist leadership, the international status of the Taipei government is enhanced. The involvement of Nationalist diplomats in overseas Chinese affairs demonstrates awareness of the fact that so long as the Nationalists can claim to speak for millions of expatriate Chinese and not merely for the people on Taiwan, Taipei's position among pro-Western nations is more secure and dignified.

In the three Southeast Asian capitals where Nationalist China is diplomatically represented—Manila, Saigon, and Bangkok—the Chinese ambassadors and their staffs are centrally concerned with gaining and retaining influence with both the overseas settlers and their host governments. The opening of a Chinese consulate in Kuala Lumpur in November 1964 marked a limited retreat from a Malaysian, formerly Malayan, unwillingness to deal politically with either Taipei or Peking. The boldness of the Chinese consul in the Malaysian capital in his relations with the local Chinese populace has yet to be determined. Presumably, he strives to avoid antagonizing his Malaysian hosts by an open effort to become a Chinese community leader. The simple fact that the Nationalists have been able to have a consul accepted in Kuala Lumpur in itself represents an international gain. The Peking Communists, to round off the picture, monopolize Chinese ambassadorships in Rangoon, Jakarta, Phnom-Penh, and, of course, Hanoi. Laos, ever perverse, attempted unsuccessfully to recognize both Peking and Taipei. Now, however, it recognizes only the former.

Conducting what is essentially a holding action, the Nationalists from 1949 on have endeavored to present themselves to the Chinese overseas as the protectors and orthodox bearers of the Chinese cultural tradition. A recurring theme in Taiwan publications succinctly states the thesis that "the anti-Communist struggle is a cultural struggle." The brilliance of Chinese thought, the masterpieces of Confucian scholarship, the beauty of Chou bronzes, Sung landscapes, or Ming porcelain are all honored under the Nationalists. At the same time, Taiwan portrays the mainland regime as philistine and barbarous.

The Nationalist withdrawal from the mainland in 1949 was anything but leisurely, yet time was somehow found during the retreat to rescue museum treasures, libraries, and archives. In exile on Taiwan, these triumphs of Chinese civilization have been preserved and displayed. It is rare to find a popular periodical from Taiwan that does not pay respect to ancient sages; poets and painters are even more frequently honored.

The Chinese written language itself has become an instrument of Nationalist cultural propaganda. On the mainland, the Communists have pushed ahead with the first phases of a revolutionary program for reform of the Chinese language. The ultimate, though perhaps visionary, goal of Peking's language reformers is abandonment of Chinese characters in favor of the Latin alphabet. Thus far, the Communist effort has resulted in the radical alteration of the forms of the more common characters. The aim has been simplification through the sharp reduction of the number of strokes employed in the characters. For example, the traditional system makes necessary the writing of 35 strokes by brush or pen to set down the four-character compound meaning *communism;* under the modified system adopted on the mainland, only 20 strokes are required. It is perhaps digressive though instructive to observe in passing that convincing arguments can be advanced to suggest that the Peking scheme for simplification actually makes many characters harder to read, remember, and distinguish because a vast number of near or actual homographs have been created.

The Nationalists will have none of this language change. No violence has been done to the writing system on Taiwan, and none is planned. The preservation of the old writing, however, is more than a negative response to a mainland innovation. Chinese characters have traditionally been much more than agents for communication and instruments for making records. For centuries, literacy has given status to those who possessed it. Little prestige can be won through mastery of the mock characters of the Communists. Men educated in the traditional writing are reluctant to adopt the new and thereby come to appear semi-literate. Beyond this consideration, there is a compelling aesthetic argument. The old characters were and, on Taiwan, remain beautiful; writing in China has long been a respected and indeed dominant art form. With simplification and eventual romanization, calligraphy would die.

The Nationalists have found in language, then, a propaganda weapon. Every printed page from Taiwan is proof that on the island, Chinese civilization is safe. By contrast, mainland publications can appear to indicate cultural irreverence in Peking. Written characters along with art treasures and literary classics are used to convince Chinese overseas that Taiwan is their ancestral country in a cultural if not in a genealogical sense.

A major difficulty confronting Taipei in its work to enlist overseas support has arisen from the fact that Taiwan was not a significant source of emigration. Few settlers in Southeast Asia can regard the island as the ancient family home. Only through emphasis on cultural integrity can the Nationalists make Taiwan seem ancestral, and that is what has been attempted. Unavoidably, however, cultural preservation is likely to appeal most strongly to the older, less progressive overseas Chinese. As a consequence, other means have been sought to attract the young and the modernizers.

As an extension of the cultural offensive designed to attract overseas youth, Taiwan has opened its educational doors. Thousands of students from abroad have gone to the Nationalist island. In 1964–65, the campus of National Taiwan University alone accommodated 2,500, and that figure represented a quarter of the university's total student body. Taiwan enjoys and makes use of certain advantages in its program to win overseas support through education. First, as the refuge of traditional learning, the island is uniquely attractive to students who seek training in classical scholarship. Second and more significant, institutions on Taiwan can provide the sort of instruction in scientific fields that is ordinarily hard to acquire in Southeast Asia, especially for Chinese restricted by quotas limiting their opportunities for university admission. Furthermore, such training is relatively free of the kind of elaborate political indoctrination fundamental to all education on the mainland. Finally, overseas Chinese students who go to Taiwan from Malaysia, Singapore, Thailand, the Philippines, and South Vietnam, where three-fourths of Southeast Asia's Chinese live, can hope to return to their homes without fear of official suspicion and hostility.

The record of economic development on Taiwan can of course impress all overseas Chinese age groups. Technological advance fosters and fulfills the expanding expectations of the young. For many older settlers whose experience and views are classically bourgeois, material progress under the Nationalists can serve as reaffirmation of the vitality of free enterprise. Investment opportunities on Taiwan for overseas capital have been productively publicized. It is officially claimed that during a decade ending in 1964, $12 million was pumped into Taiwan's industrialization by expatriate Chinese.[1] The attraction of overseas funds to the island serves a twofold purpose: the economic base of the Nationalists is made more secure, and Chinese abroad are shown that the Kuomintang is capable of leading modernization. Economic achievements rank with cultural preservation as favored subjects for propaganda presentation.

Taiwan publications reaching overseas readers devote substantial space to discussions of the international status of Nationalist China. These efforts center on two aspects of Taipei's relations abroad. First, considerable publicity is given to the visits of foreign notables. Distinguished and not so distinguished guests of the Nationalists invariably are introduced to the overseas Chinese through articles and photographs. It is a rare generalized periodical from Taiwan that does not contain descriptions of the state visits of foreign royalty, political figures, and others. Receptions held for obscure, inconsequential touring persons and groups are solemnly reported. When a guest of genuine world stature turns up, the Nationalist press treats the event as monumental and pivotal. All this publicity is clearly designed to calm fears that Taiwan is not a respected world power.

A second feature of the Nationalist press emphasis on international prestige directly involves the overseas Chinese. All settlers abroad are called to come visit "the ancestral land," that is, Taiwan. And when overseas people respond to the invitation, as did some 13,000 in 1964,[2] hospitality and publicity await them. Signs at the Taipei airport welcome the visitors "home." In the hills near the Nationalist capital, a hostel to shelter touring expatriates is provided by the Overseas Chinese Affairs Commission, the agency responsible for the maintenance of official links between the government in Taipei and the settlers. The activity surrounding Chinese visitors from abroad increases each year in the early fall when special festivities are planned in connection with the October 10 anniversary of the 1911 Revolution and, sometimes as an added

[1] *Free China Weekly*, v. 2, no. 16, December 13, 1964.
[2] Same, v. 2, no. 20, January 10, 1965.

treat, the October 31 birthday of Chiang Kai-shek. Overseas Chinese representatives review and march in the annual parade on October 10, and the press unfailingly reports that participation. The excitement of many visitors is augmented by the appearance of their names in the newspapers. It all must be quite intoxicating for the unassuming men, typically well into or beyond middle age, who make the pilgrimage. For a time, freed from the grocery store in Peru or the wholesale house in Thailand, these men become celebrities.

More meaningful and possibly more lasting than the thrill of the trip is the faith generated among visitors in the viability of Nationalist China. The military and aerial might paraded on October 10, the urban vigor of Taipei, and the prosperity of the countryside are convincing. It is hard from a remote vantage point not to imagine Taiwan to be beleaguered and impoverished. On the island itself, however, the climate of confidence and the sense of progress strike all visitors. Life appears normal; the future seems not without hope. Above all, the Nationalists earnestly work to win overseas Chinese hearts.

The Communist Effort

The Communists in Peking initially took over the techniques and purposes established by the Kuomintang in overseas Chinese affairs. In the first years after their mainland victory, the Communists assiduously sought to generate support among the settlers abroad. Students and visitors were urged to go to China; ancient culture was respected; overseas capital was attracted; strong support for the overseas Chinese in their difficulties with host governments was promised. In Communist publications designed for overseas consumption in the first years after 1949, it is hard to find much that is distinctive, although marked emphases are perceptible. Peking laid heavy stress on appeals to Chinese nationalism among expatriates and on evidence of China's growing economic and political strength.

The claim that the Communists had liberated China from imperialism, it should be noted, figured prominently in the propaganda directed to the Chinese abroad. The companion claim that China had also achieved liberation from semi-feudalism, however, received less space in publications for export than in those for domestic consumption. Landlordism in China had not been a source of grief to the Chinese overseas. In fact, much overseas capital had been remitted to support relatives in rural comfort, and it was traditional for Chinese expatriates to dream of an old age made serene and dignified through the ownership of land in the native village. The Communists were at first careful not to frighten the overseas Chinese by redistributing their holdings of land, but it was soon clear that the future would give no respected place to the repatriated, idle squire.

China's entry into the Korean War a little more than a year after the establishment of the People's Republic brought intensification of the nationalistic stress. The conflict was portrayed as a struggle between the Korean people, aided by unselfish Chinese volunteers, and the forces of imperialism. Inoffensive Asians were resisting Western savagery. When Peking accused the Americans of employing germ warfare, the racism in Chinese Communist writings emerged more unashamedly. The response of overseas Chinese audiences cannot be measured, yet the persistence and volume of the propaganda offensive no doubt indicate some success. It is surely true that the charge of bacteriological warfare must have seemed substantiated to many by the elaborate documentation created to support it. The crude photographs and the clumsy reports were patently fraudulent to objective scientific specialists, but the effort had not been made in their behalf.

The end of the war did not bring an end to strident nationalism. Indeed, the mainland press interpreted the conclusion of hostilities as a triumph of Asian arms. To even the skeptical among the overseas Chinese, it was evident that the West had not won, and that in itself broke a pattern of more than a century's duration. The Indochina war and its termination at Geneva provided the same sort of grist for the Peking mill. Asians were proclaimed to be liberating themselves, and China was cited as the example and the inspiration for their efforts. The same boast is now repeated in reports on the war in Vietnam.

The later break between Communist China and the Soviet Union removed a blemish from the nationalistic complexion of the Peking press. No longer was there a need to pay homage to the Russian elder brother and thereby dilute Chinese chauvinism. The cult of Maoism could flourish, and the Maoist claim to Communist leadership and orthodoxy is, after all, fundamentally an expression of Chinese nationalism. To some Southeast Asian Chinese, the assertion of independence by Peking must have seemed proof of the power and confirmation of the prestige of the People's Republic.

Some years ago, an officer of the U.S. Information Service in a Southeast Asian capital told the present writer that the most effective technique in the campaign of his agency to counter communism among the overseas Chinese consisted simply of publicizing photographs of mainland China parades of children carrying huge pictures of Soviet, only Soviet, leaders. The implication that the People's Republic was not fully sovereign was reportedly sensed by many. No such embarrassment to Peking would be possible today. The Maoist personality cult dramatizes the Chinese essence of the mainland party and regime. Presumably, the anticipated overseas Chinese response was not a matter of central concern in the making of the decisions leading to the Sino-Soviet rupture and the beatification of Mao Tse-tung, yet the unearned increment in propaganda strength thus produced has surely been exploited.

In opposition to this conclusion is the suggestion that the overseas Chinese have been disillusioned by the events leading to and surrounding the Peking–Moscow split. Struggle between the two giants, it is argued, exposes the clay feet of international communism and the scientific poverty of Marxism. There is validity in such an analysis if it is to measure the response of a sophisticated and uninvolved audience, but the thesis is false if it is used to predict overseas Chinese reactions. Many Chinese abroad see Peking's intransigence and isolation as victories of Chinese nationalism. Those sympathetic to the People's Republic are unlikely to consider that denied Russian support, China is weakened; to them, China's independence proves her strength.

Since the break between Peking and Moscow, two events have

vastly added to the confidence of those who believe that the Maoist course is right. First there was China's singlehanded and rather effortless military humbling of India. Second came China's entry into the select club of nuclear powers. For the moment, the West is comforted by the knowledge that Chinese atomic devices have been somewhat primitive and that the People's Republic is years behind in the technology of delivery systems. It must be assumed, however, that to most—if not all—overseas Chinese, China has now become a great power in the mid-twentieth-century meaning of the term. The military implications of Peking's nuclear success may presently be slight; the political consequences are immeasurable.

Periodicals, books, and radio transmissions announce Chinese Communist successes. Newspapers frankly favorable to Peking have been relatively insignificant; where the great majority of the overseas Chinese are situated, straight Communist-line journals would be banned. A daily sympathetic to Peking, *Sin Po,* was once a force in Indonesia, but state control of the press in that country interrupted its publication. No other mass-circulation Chinese paper of Communist leanings has been equally conspicuous in Southeast Asia, but that fact has not meant that news made in China receives no attention.

Some Chinese newspapers in the region have been swayed toward Peking in two ways. First, there have been reporters and editors inclined to give extensive coverage to mainland China's domestic and international gains. Whether these men have been motivated by Chinese chauvinism or by a simple commercial desire to satisfy the demands of their readers is not to be judged and is, in fact, of little consequence. The point is that selective news coverage can favor mainland China—except where rigorous press censorship operates, as in Saigon or Bangkok.

The second journalistic weapon of Peking is the New China News Agency. Chinese-language papers in Southeast Asia rarely maintain correspondents abroad. As a result, nearly all foreign news comes from the various wire services. For example, it has been the practice in Singapore for Chinese dailies to print stories from Reuters, the New China News Agency, the U.S. Information Service, and other sources. Since the public expects reporting on

China, news from Peking is given space. In extreme situations, as in Indonesia (at least until October 1965), virtually all foreign news reached both overseas Chinese and indigenous readers over Chinese Communist wires.

Observers of Communist information programs have been impressed by the wisdom of schemes to spread propaganda through the medium of inexpensive magazines and books. Obviously sold at a loss, such publications can reach a grateful public. Typically, readers have limited financial means and are youthful. One has only to visit a bookstore selling mainland Chinese publications to see that most customers are shabby and young. Peking caters to precisely the group within which it can best hope to find converts.

The shops handling Chinese Communist books and periodicals by no means stock only the dry and the doctrinaire. Noisy propaganda would be outlawed in most countries in any case. Browsing among the mainland Chinese selections, one normally uncovers innocuous items such as reproductions of art treasures, dictionaries, maps, textbooks, and magazines on sports. If, as until recently in Jakarta, it is permitted, the dealer will also display the writings of the Maoist sages. It would seem that the chief advantages of these commercial ventures are in strengthening cultural bonds between the overseas Chinese and mainland China and in earning the thanks of customers skilled at recognizing a bargain.

If the excellence of reception in Southeast Asia and the number of hours programmed are measures, then it is clear that Peking believes in the efficacy of propaganda by radio. Short-wave broadcasts in the many Chinese and indigenous languages blanket the region. Punctuated hourly with the opening bars of "Arise," the Chinese Communist anthem, programs of news, commentary, and music travel tropical air waves. An overseas Chinese seeking to improve his Mandarin can get hours of free, flawless instruction; those ignorant of that language can listen to much the same fare in a regional Chinese or Southeast Asian tongue. The splendor of China, not of Communist ideology, is the constant theme. The simple fact that Peking can transmit its messages with efficiency and in such volume is itself proof of Chinese technological advance. No head count of listeners can be made, but the compact, inexpensive radio would seem to be bringing about a revolution in communications. What the printed page did for the West a couple of centuries ago may be accomplished today by the transistor.

Evidence of mainland material progress less awesome than a military invasion or an atomic blast is presented to the overseas Chinese in great volume. Real or imagined advances in agricultural output and manufacturing are reported in virtually every mainland broadcast or publication directed southward. Possibly more influential than words are the Chinese products now available in many Southeast Asian markets. Chinese exports are spreading, depending upon local demand and import regulations, through much of the region. Textiles, sewing machines, flashlights, bicycles, radio sets, and scores of other items formerly made only in the West or Japan now come from mainland China. To overseas Chinese merchants and consumers, the message seems clear: China is now advancing industrially. The usual shoddy inferiority of Chinese exports and the general overseas Chinese awareness of harsh living standards on the mainland do not necessarily diminish pride in the industrial achievements of the People's Republic. Since the exports tangibly and daily remind great numbers of overseas settlers of economic accomplishments on the mainland, undershirts and cooking utensils may well be as convincing as propaganda instruments as atomic tests in China's far west or a triumph of arms in the remote Himalayas.

Communist China's foreign-aid programs are not specifically designed to impress settlers abroad, but in countries where Peking supports conspicuous projects, such as in Cambodia, the propaganda impact on the overseas Chinese must be considerable. Like trade, aid from the mainland symbolizes the material rise of the People's Republic. Not long ago, it can be reasoned, China was a pauper in need of foreign help; today she can assist others. The burden imposed on the Chinese people and the modest scale of the aid programs may not always get due consideration.

To further her campaign to attain international eminence, the People's Republic also pays scrupulous attention to the niceties of state hospitality. Like Taipei, Peking devotes a remarkable amount of space in its publications to reporting the reception of foreign dignitaries. Few statesmen or delegations on tour to the mainland are too obscure to be denied a state welcome on a grand scale and detailed press coverage of their entertainment. Similarly, the foreign travels of representatives of the People's Republic are treated as matters of prime news value. The obvious object of the voluminous and often tedious reporting is to remind Chinese at home and overseas that their country is a leading power.

Another parallel between Peking and Taipei propaganda offerings to the overseas Chinese can be seen in the cultural area. Both governments display pride in China's artistic grandeur. As has been pointed out previously, the Nationalists claim to be the legitimate sons and defenders of a superb cultural heritage. The Communists at first glance seem to be at a disadvantage in several respects. The sages and doctrines of Confucianism must be banished as "feudal"; some writers and poets are condemned as degenerate; art that somehow cannot be included in the tradition of the masses is out of favor. By and large, however, the critics on the mainland have been broad-minded and selectively iconoclastic. Thus, for example, it has been possible to classify Buddhist cave paintings as expressions of popular art; and until the recent remolding campaign began, the opera prospered under Mao although many plots seemed to honor patently reactionary generals and emperors. It has been suggested by observers of the Southeast Asian scene, incidentally, that the most potent propaganda sent to the overseas Chinese from the mainland takes the form of filmed versions of classical operas from Peking and provincial stages. Such a film in a South China regional language played to packed houses in Singapore for many weeks not long ago. No overt propaganda was offered, yet there was the implication that in the People's Republic, theatrical traditions and regional subcultures are respected. In such ways, the Communists are able to counter the charge of cultural boorishness.

Although the Nationalists and Communists base their appeals on the same broad cultural foundation, Peking enjoys the unique possession of certain assets. Foremost is the Communist hold on the homeland of Chinese civilization. Both the spirit and the substance of the Communists' propaganda through culture are enriched. Mao, not Chiang, rules the mountains and streams of the revered landscape painters and the inspirational locales of the honored poets. In the golden age of Chinese civilization, the island of Taiwan was barren of intellectual and artistic achievements.

Furthermore, archaeological sites and monuments of architecture could not be moved across the Taiwan Strait in 1949; nor did the bulk of China's museum treasures go with the retreating Nationalists. The majority of China's artists, musicians, and singers stayed on the mainland. It is thus impossible to determine which side in the Chinese struggle is stronger culturally. Taiwan respects tradition; the mainland is the home and in large measure the repository of that tradition.

Peking sends two new and meaningful messages to the overseas Chinese. Both are directly the result of the wish and the campaign of the People's Republic to court the leadership of those states ordinarily designated neutralist—that is, Burma, Cambodia, and, until recently, Indonesia. The settlers abroad are told that they ought to become loyal naturalized citizens of their tropical homes; if such an accommodation proves impossible, those overseas Chinese who face deportation are promised sanctuary on the mainland. These two revolutionary departures from an official Chinese stand taken more than sixty years ago are clear expressions of Mao's resolve to avoid responsibility for the overseas Chinese irritant in countries where grand strategy can be served through seeking the friendship of nationalist leaders. The Chinese abroad, from the perspective of Peking, are often an embarrassment and invariably expendable.

Reversal of the established Chinese policy on citizenship has been given substance through treaties based upon an exchange initially undertaken between Chou En-lai and Indonesian authorities a decade ago. As proof of her desire for international amity, China dropped the claim that all persons born of Chinese fathers anywhere in the world and their descendants through the male line over limitless generations were Chinese citizens. Under the new principle, overseas Chinese ought to be able to acquire citizenship in their lands of birth or residence. No longer would complex disputes over dual nationality unsettle relations between China and her neighbors. The propaganda to the Chinese abroad has not only pointed out the possibility of changing allegiance where feasible but regularly encouraged the expatriates to alienate themselves legally.

The conciliatory moves of the People's Republic in the matter of citizenship by no means stilled the quarrels between the overseas Chinese and their hosts. Particularly in Indonesia, the settlers have experienced cruel pressure from the government and violence from mobs. As a consequence, up to 100,000 overseas Chinese have had to seek refuge on the mainland.[3] The bitter exchange between Peking and Jakarta prior to the exodus establishes that the Communist regime at first sought to prevent expulsion. Once repatriation became the only way for many expatriates to escape suffering and for Peking to avoid antagonizing Sukarno, machinery was devised to transport and resettle the displaced people. Special communities of returned overseas Chinese were set up on Hainan island, in Yunnan, and elsewhere in southern China. It is likely that the majority of the "returnees" had never seen China before, since emigration had been restricted for three decades. Moreover, those who had originated on the mainland in most cases were resettled in places unknown to them or their ancestors. Beyond these difficulties, the repatriates have had to try to remake their minds in order to blend into the ideological scenery. If one judges by mainland publications, the returned Chinese have been hard to handle. Recently, for example, an editorial designed to guide repatriates toward purity warns against their tendency to "center their interests around the individual, one-sidedly asking the State for special consideration or for personal freedoms which are detrimental to the collective interest." Salvation, of course, is to be found through "learning from the People's Liberation Army" to become "red and expert." [4] Repatriation clearly has been a mass marriage of inconvenience. The program must seem less than ideal to many

[3] In the past decade and a half, 200,000 Chinese have repatriated themselves. About half this number left Indonesia about 1960; most of the others reached China in the early years of Communist rule. See Ma Ch'ang-tsung, "State Farms for Returned Overseas Chinese," *China Monthly* (Hong Kong United Research Institute), no. 2, February 1, 1965, p. 9.

[4] *Ch'iao-wu-pao* [*Overseas Chinese Affairs Journal*] (Peking), no. 6, December 1964.

repatriates and to the officials responsible, yet there is no alternative. Peking, in any case, makes proud propaganda use of its humanitarian record both to impress the overseas Chinese and to reassure Southeast Asian friends.

On matters of citizenship and repatriation, it can be noted that Taipei has followed Peking in a limited and grudging manner. The Nationalists have now come to acknowledge the right of a man to change his nationality, but no active effort is made to broadcast this departure from tradition. Although systematic investigation of the Nationalist stand on citizenship and its consequences has not been made, it appears that the older leadership in Taipei still adheres to a belief in the feasibility of dual nationality.

The repatriation of overseas Chinese to Taiwan is by no means favored by the Nationalist government. Some persons have come from abroad to seek haven on the island, but ordinarily Taipei argues that there is no room for repatriates. Even possession of a Nationalist passport is no guarantee of admission. The government on Taiwan must come close to being unique in claiming the right to deny entry onto its territory to its own citizens. A rather embarrassing diplomatic dialogue between Manila and Taipei went on for some years over this issue. The Philippine government planned to deport Nationalist Chinese who overstayed their Philippine visas, but Taiwan refused to admit them.

Similarities and Differences

It is perhaps useful at this point to sum up the similarities and differences between the Communists and the Nationalists in the matter of propaganda directed to the overseas Chinese. Both sides lay claim to custody over China's cultural legacy, although the claims differ in definition and justification. Peking and Taipei share a wish to appear materially progressive and internationally respected. The two regimes are distinct from each other most notably with regard to citizenship and repatriation. Although it might seem that the distinction in these concerns is one of degree rather than kind, the fact is that Peking actively employs its policies on the two issues to serve larger political ends while Taipei seeks to avoid involvement in nationality conflicts and opens its doors with great reluctance. The difference in form between the Communist and the Nationalist positions on citizenship and repatriation thus actually has produced contrasting programs.

Finally, it should be stressed that there is little overt political propaganda aimed at the Chinese abroad. Although the Communist or Nationalist actions and statements may conceivably be seen in an ideological context, Peking is not blatantly seeking Communist converts, nor is Taipei conducting a Kuomintang membership drive among the overseas Chinese. Both appeal to the nationalism of the settlers in Southeast Asia; the recruitment of disciplined political followers is an underground operation only incidentally dependent upon open propaganda.

Communist China's efforts to use overseas Chinese power for the attainment of political ends have thus far been restricted in both scope and achievement. Peking, it is true, now openly asks for help against the governments in Saigon and Kuala Lumpur, currently at the head of its black list. Chinese in South Vietnam have been urged to join the Communists' National Liberation Front to "struggle against the United States imperialist aggressors." [5] On the occasion of the fifteenth anniversary of the founding of the People's Republic in 1964, Radio Peking stated:

We are watching closely the persecution of the people of Chinese origin in Malaya by U.S. imperialism and old and neo-colonialism in collusion with the Rahman clique. We hope that overseas Chinese in Malaya and Singapore unite closely with local people of various nationalities to oppose imperialism and smash the schemes of imperialism and reactionaries in creating racial disputes, spreading an anti-China atmosphere, and suppressing the people's anti-imperialist struggle.

Continuing, the broadcast somewhat irrelevantly added:

We are extremely indignant over the persecution of Chinese nationals by the Indian government. We resolutely demand the release of the several hundred Chinese nationals who are being detained by the Indian government.[6]

[5] *The New York Times,* June 16, 1965.
[6] *Ch'iao-wu-pao,* cited, no. 5, October 1964.

Only the Chinese in countries hostile to the People's Republic, however, are called upon to be disobedient to their governments. Elsewhere, Chinese are encouraged to be inconspicuous, decent settlers. Not the least of the short-run dividends enjoyed by Peking's Southeast Asian friends, notably Sukarno, Ne Win, and Sihanouk, has been the public tractability of the pro-Communist Chinese under their rule.

In Malaysia, it appears that Communist China has tried most diligently to work through fronts. Subversion in that country, after all, is particularly inviting. The peninsula has a recent history of Chinese Communist insurrection, and Singapore for some years had seemed to be ripening for Communist harvest. Intercommunal divisions are capable of igniting civil disorder. By seeking to sabotage Malaysia, Peking supported the confrontation policy of Sukarno, its most powerful friend. Finally, and perhaps decisively, the full success of the Malaysian experiment could have served to inspire wavering Southeast Asian countries to resist the attraction of the Maoist path to material progress.

It is neither the purpose nor the right of this study to indict individuals or parties hostile to Malaysia on charges of Communist subversion. However, the bald fact is that there was an unmistakable similarity between the Peking line and the anti-Malaysia positions of the far left in that new country. Participants in the overseas Chinese-dominated Barisan Sosialis of Singapore, the Socialist Front of Malaya, and the Sarawak United People's Party may honestly have been suspicious of the aims and feasibility of Malaysia; but the antipathy of elements within those parties toward the constitution of Malaysia was in fact distressingly like that of Communist China.

The tie between Peking and its overseas sympathizers has been most apparent in fronts like the Sarawak Farmers Association, reportedly set up by the Chinese Communists and now officially proscribed. Fearing rural insurrection near Kuching, the authorities have recently forced ethnic Chinese in one area to move into resettlement centers watched by the police and insulated against the Communists. As Sarawak has been the most troubled war zone in the Malaysian-Indonesian contest, the government is particularly cautious. On the other hand, the Chinese Communists have been especially active and influential among the rural Chinese of the state. In any case, the lessons of Sarawak are instructive and ominous. The techniques of the front organization can serve the Communists wherever substantial numbers of discontented overseas Chinese, little assimilated to the local society, are to be found. As the experience of the Malayan Emergency has shown, largely self-contained Chinese rural settlements seem uniquely susceptible to manipulation by Communist fronts.

Exerting influence among businessmen, who are at the other end of the overseas Chinese social order from the farmers, are the Bank of China and the agents of mainland China's state trading companies. Branches of the bank were understandably denied licenses to open in anti-Communist Thailand, South Vietnam, or the Philippines. The nationalization of banking in Burma and the pattern of state control in Indonesia have now excluded the bank there as well. Until Singapore seceded from Malaysia, the authorities had planned to close the bank's last Southeast Asian office. Thus, the banking arm of Peking is actually weak and vulnerable.

Where the bank has been active, Chinese business communities have felt its local power. In particular, policies on credit extension are reported to have been politically determined. For example, a merchant seeking a loan would be more hospitably received at the bank if he sought credit to finance the import of Chinese Communist goods. Similarly, contributions to those Chinese community projects blessed by the Communists, such as a pro-Peking school, could be evidence of good credit standing.

Representatives of Chinese Communist export-import enterprises, such as officials of the Bank of China, can make or break some overseas Chinese merchants. Where trade with China is significant, as in Singapore or Indonesia, maintaining harmony with Peking's commercial agents can be exceedingly good business for merchants wishing to make a sale. Likewise, the opportunity to buy the exports of the Chinese mainland on good terms can be reserved to those overseas Chinese dealers whose personal political lives are unblemished according to Communist standards. No statistics will reveal the proportion of Sino-Southeast Asian trade serving political ends. Neither the Communists nor their overseas Chinese commercial associates are likely to publicize that aspect of the relationship, yet the frequency of reports and rumors of the kinds of pressure described points to extensive use of trade as a political tool.

Where the Communists have sought to build up a loyal, disciplined overseas Chinese following, the young and their schools have received much attention. The revolutionary potential of the Chinese of Southeast Asia, if it is in fact strong, is likely to be found among the youthful. The chief recruiting agencies of the Clandestine Communist Organization in Sarawak, for example, have been those schools under Communist sway. In Singapore, Nanyang University, the only Chinese university in Southeast Asia, long experienced infiltration by Communist sympathizers. Nanyang never came under full Maoist domination, nor is it likely that the student body ever became largely Communist in its loyalties. Nevertheless, pro-Peking youths were the campus activists who set the political tone of the institution and alarmed the Singapore police. Now, under a reorganized administration, the university is seeking to achieve its original purpose of meeting overseas Chinese needs in higher education.

In Cambodia, owing to the warmth of that country's relationship with China, it was uniquely easy for men in sympathy with Peking to assume leadership over the various local Chinese community enterprises. Schools, merchants' associations, and communal organizations became publicly oriented toward Communist China. That development, however, is not necessarily as sinister as it might seem, for it was precisely because of the overseas Chinese desire to win favor with a popular, strong ruler, Prince Sihanouk, that the moves were made. That is, even where the Communists have won out, the victory was possible primarily because the overseas Chinese were bending to local political circumstances. More and more, the Chinese of Southeast Asia are getting into step with the changes in their adopted countries. They are moving toward political assimilation. It is to that tendency and to the optimism it inspires that the following chapter will turn.

CHAPTER FIVE

Causes and Signs of Change

Great events over the past three and a half decades have transformed overseas Chinese life. Coming in uninterrupted succession, depression, war, revolution, and independence have made Southeast Asia barely recognizable by the measures of a generation ago. The position and the outlook of the Chinese in the region have been profoundly and irreversibly affected. Recent changes and developments still in process are of course not necessarily understood or even acknowledged by the participants. In the matter of men's responses to historical turns, proximity by no means insures perception. Just as Louis XVI is supposed to have recorded in his diary that nothing happened on the day the Bastille fell, many Chinese in Southeast Asia appear unable to grasp what is taking place. That much has changed is known by all, but the nature and implications of the changes are not easily sensed. It is appropriate here to attempt to describe and analyze tentatively the sources and consequences of the current evolution of the overseas Chinese.

Isolation from China

Coming thirty years after the birth of nationalism among the Chinese abroad, the world depression of the interwar era dramatically recast overseas Chinese patterns by stifling immigration. Indeed, it may in due course be concluded that the stemming of the torrent of immigrants was as crucial in the history of the overseas Chinese as their nationalist awakening. Political orientation toward China was the product of nationalism; overseas Chinese assimilation [1] within Southeast Asia may well result from the cutting off of the flow of new immigrants to refresh the expatriate communities.

Although there is uncertainty over the date of the arrival of the first Chinese in Southeast Asia, as has already been noted, the period of mass immigration into the region can be conveniently defined. From the start of an age of vast economic development around the middle of the nineteenth century until the post-1929 depression brought commercial contraction and the shrinking of markets for tropical exports, there was a steady demand for Chinese immigrant labor in much of the area. As a consequence of the global economic collapse, however, Chinese workers overnight found their welcome worn out. The absence of jobs caused prospective emigrants to stay home in their villages where, despite the poverty, there was a degree of security, however pitiful. Agents no longer scoured Kwangtung and Fukien to recruit labor. Perhaps of the least immediate importance, though in the long run universally and firmly established, were the curbs and prohibitions on immigration enforced by the governments of Southeast Asia. Not only were immigrants from China unwelcome; at home, few Chinese found sufficient reason to make the trip. In comparison to the export economies of Southeast Asia, China was little touched by the depression. There subsistence agriculture remained much the same despite the violence done to world prices and international trade.

Well before the depression was over, war came to South China and soon to Southeast Asia. The hazards or impossibility of wartime travel automatically ruled out the revival of immigration.

---

[1] The term *assimilation* has a range of meanings. When used in this study, it refers to the process by which overseas Chinese become oriented toward their Southeast Asian homelands. For clarity, *political assimilation* will be used to describe the participation of Chinese in government and politics, and *cultural assimilation* will be used to refer to broader and more profound acculturation. *Absorption* means the virtual disappearance of overseas Chinese as a distinct ethnic entity. All these developments can be observed in Southeast Asia; local circumstances control the nature, the extent, and the pace of change.

In any case, under Japanese rule Southeast Asia was economically dead. Peace did not bring a restoration of immigration on a politically significant scale. In some places, it was years before recovery from the destruction and decay of the war opened job opportunities. Only token numbers of Chinese could slip through the barriers to immigration initially erected for economic protection in the depression period and subsequently maintained as an expression of nationalism. Four years after the defeat of Japan, China came under Communist control. The consequences with respect to immigration were predictable. The People's Republic normally kept its citizens inside; foreign immigration controls often acquired new teeth as instruments for checking Communist influence.

In these ways, large transfusions of fresh Chinese blood have been denied Southeast Asia for a generation. A sort of anemia must result, although the degree to which the overseas Chinese have lost communal vigor is uncertain and must vary from place to place. The momentous fact remains that with the possible exception of Burma, where clandestine immigration has been substantial, no country in the region has a large proportion of China-born settlers. In all places, the Chinese of local origin are in heavy majority. When one considers that the runaway birth rate of the overseas Chinese has produced an incredibly young population, one can more readily appreciate the tiny size of the China-born minority. In Singapore, for example, about half the inhabitants of Chinese ancestry are under fifteen years of age. Virtually none of these youngsters is an alien by birth, and their parents are likely to have no personal memory of China.

This situation may or may not give rise to a lessening of emotional attachment to China. As has been pointed out, youthful Chinese of Southeast Asian birth may develop a starved curiosity about China and thus a seemingly irrational devotion to Chinese political symbols and cultural achievements.[2] The fact remains, however, that the overseas Chinese are in the midst of a demographic revolution and are physically cut off from China as never before.

[2] T'ien Ju-k'ang, *The Chinese of Sarawak* (London: London School of Economics, 1953), *passim*.

The current isolation of the Chinese abroad is reinforced by developments more recent and nearly as fundamental as the immigrant drought. In the area of education, the settlers are largely cut off from China as the result of a quarter of a century of turmoil. The wars and revolutions which all but halted the migration of labor were equally injurious to Chinese educational endeavors in Southeast Asia. No longer could overseas students easily make the scholastic pilgrimage to the ancestral land, nor could many teachers move south to staff expatriate schools. From the opening of the century until the final explosion of Japanese aggression in 1937, countless overseas parents had come to regard schooling in China as a means for their children to advance themselves economically through modern training and socially through the acquisition of proper Chinese culture. Career goals and nationalism were thus linked and served. The sending of children to China demonstrated a man's concern for the welfare of his sons as well as the depth and sincerity of his attachment to the nation and culture of China.

The recruitment of teachers in China to staff overseas schools was similarly an expression of both nationalism and intellectual commitment. The instructors brought south were prized for their mastery of Mandarin and for their ability within the classroom to use what were thought to be the latest and most effective teaching methods and texts. Had the directors of the overseas schools been content to provide children with instructions in the rudiments of arithmetic and the elementary written Chinese that met the daily needs of most of their fathers, there would have been small demand for teachers and books from China and little willingness to spend the sizable sums necessary for advanced, nationalistic education.

In the immediate postwar years a few mainland teachers made their way south, and after 1949 some Chinese political refugees managed to establish themselves in Southeast Asian teaching posts. However, travel restrictions and in some places official hostility toward Chinese education obstructed the flow of teachers. Increasingly, schools had to rely on the young products of the overseas systems for personnel. The most conspicuous inadequacy of those trained locally is their often rather bizarre handling of spoken Mandarin. There have sprung up stories, some no doubt true, to illustrate the consequences of learning the language through instructors themselves several removes from its homeland. It has been reported, for example, that linguistically pure visitors on occasion require the services of an interpreter able to put overseas schoolboy Mandarin into an approximation of the real thing. This result of the shortage of China-born teachers is most obvious in areas where the pressures of government on Chinese education and official curbs on immigration have been strong.

In the sense that an enthusiastic initial response was generated among the Chinese settlers, the Communists were successful in a campaign begun shortly after the establishment of the People's Republic to attract overseas students to the mainland. That the program has since all but disintegrated does not erase the fact that nationalism combined with a yearning for education prompted an estimated 60,000 youths, 40,000 of them in the 1953–55 period alone, to seek training under the Communists. Indonesia and what are now Malaysia and Singapore contributed the bulk of the students, but all Southeast Asia was represented.[3]

Two sets of reasons for the eventual failure of Peking-sponsored education on the mainland can be found. To begin with, many of the young people who hopefully went north in the early 1950s are banned from returning home. The various Southeast Asian countries have feared, not surprisingly, that students returning from the People's Republic would be subversive agents for communism and expanding Chinese power, for all those schooled under the auspices of Peking inevitably have been exposed to Maoist indoctrination. Furthermore, as men trained on the mainland might well have acquired technical and professional skills that would give them an upper hand in competition for jobs back home, their exclusion was no doubt also a function of Southeast Asian nationalism. Understandably, the number of overseas students now willing to go to the People's Republic and able to secure parental permission to exile themselves has shrunk.

Trouble also arose on the mainland. The bourgeois and exotic backgrounds of the students from abroad reportedly made them

[3] Ch'iao Chien-shen, "Education of Returned Overseas Chinese," *China Monthly* (Hong Kong Union Research Institute), no. 2, February 1, 1965, p. 18.

suspect. Segregation of overseas students from their more trust-worthy mainland classmates was common. There was disillusion-ment among the imported scholars over being regarded as un-reliable and in fact not fully Chinese. An inadequate command of Mandarin and of Chinese characters was a handicap for some. Disappointment with the kind of education offered was felt by those who had come to acquire a profession but were merely taught a trade. The general drabness of life in a mainland institu-tion is said to have weighed heavily. Restless, homesick, dis-enchanted, several thousand overseas students have left the Peo-ple's Republic. Most of these have had no choice but to subsist, as do so many others as refugees, in Hong Kong. Perhaps a most telling propaganda blow against Communist China would be struck if these forlorn former students could return to South-east Asia to publicize their experiences.

As was mentioned earlier, the Chinese Nationalists on Taiwan, within the limits of their overtaxed educational establishment, have carried on the tradition of inviting overseas students to "come home." The size of Taiwan and the strain put upon the schools and universities there by the local population explosion make it impossible for more than a small though symbolic proportion of overseas youth to study on Taiwan. Yet Nationalist China has now come close to monopolizing the education in a Chinese setting of overseas students who will return home, often to teach in schools in Southeast Asia.

The physical separation of the overseas Chinese from China is also evident in the sharp drop in voluntary repatriation in recent decades. There was a time when return to the native village was the dream of most immigrants; the dream has now evaporated. Except for those forcibly expelled from Sukarno's Indonesia, al-most no expatriate now retires to China after a lifetime of foreign toil. The disruptions of war and revolution which halted the northward travel of students to the mainland were equally destruc-tive to the plans of sojourners for resettlement in their birthplaces. After the Communists established their pattern for the total organ-ization of Chinese life, there was no familiar and comfortable niche in the communalized villages for aging sons back from the outside world. In earlier times, idleness was a luxury to be sought and respected. The returned overseas Chinese who could afford to lead the leisurely life of the rural gentry was viewed as a success by his neighbors, and his status was high. The prestige of such leisure in old China was of course symbolized by uncut fingernails, the cheapest signs of affluence ever devised, as John Fairbank has wittily observed.[4] There are no long nails in the People's Republic, and there is little place for those who would have affected them in an earlier age.

As something of a footnote, it can be pointed out that the barriers to repatriation for the living are supplemented by restrictions on the shipment of the dead to China for burial. The Communist authorities have concluded, quite rationally in economic terms, that much prime land was formerly taken out of agricultural production and used for the erection of tombs; therefore, they have destroyed or relocated old graves and have not permitted new ones to be placed in fertile fields. Communal burial is favored; ostentatious funerals are impossible. As a consequence, deceased expatriates are no longer returned to ancestral villages for burial. Thousands of overseas Chinese coffins have been stored abroad for eventual shipment home, but the great majority of expatriates have come to anticipate burial overseas. The tie between the Chinese abroad and their ancestors thus decreasingly involves emotional and filial attachment to tombs on the mainland. Anyone who has observed the faithfulness with which Chinese annually visit and tend family graves will sense the significance of the change in burial preferences. Even beyond the grave, the overseas Chinese do not fit into the Chinese Communist scheme.

Short trips to the mainland remain possible and indeed popular for some Chinese abroad. If their credentials are acceptable to Peking and if the governments of their overseas homes tolerate travel to and from Communist China, tourists are able to visit relatives and see the sights in the People's Republic. In Singapore, for example, an industry grew up to provide for such travel. Agents sell packaged tours which take care of all the documentary, travel, and living arrangements involved in a trip. Tour leaders specializing in this service normally accompany groups of travelers. Superficial observation leads the present writer to believe that the bulk of the tourists are in or past middle age. Such persons are likely to

[4] John K. Fairbank, *The United States and China* (Cambridge: Harvard University Press, 1959), p. 43.

be China-born, to have relatives on the mainland, and to be regarded as safely apolitical by the authorities at both ends of the journey. The volume of travel is limited, and the impact made by returning tourists on their expatriate communities cannot be greatly influential. Yet this link between China and parts of Southeast Asia survives for the present.

Traditionally, the overseas Chinese have tried to send more than themselves or their corpses to China. Enormous sums of money earned and saved abroad were transmitted to and invested in the ancestral land. No more tangible expression of attachment to the homeland and family existed. For years, China's balance of international payments was kept in equilibrium by overseas remittances offsetting deficits in exports. Today, when the People's Republic, most unashamedly in her relations with Hong Kong, displays a hunger for foreign exchange, overseas Chinese remittances are falling off. As the demands of family and the strength of individual commitments fade, fewer expatriates feel obliged to meet receding obligations. Not only the fact of physical separation but the perniciousness of the policies of the People's Republic have cut remittances. Efforts to extort money from the settlers abroad through not always subtle suggestions that contributors' relatives on the mainland could expect special consideration were extensively reported in the first years of the Communist regime. Although it is impossible to verify stories of Peking pressure on expatriates in the form of threats to kinfolk back in the ancestral village, the fact is that there was not only much discussion of this kind of blackmail among the overseas Chinese but a widespread belief in the truth of the charges. The revulsion which ensued no doubt contributed to an unwillingness to remit funds. In more recent years, Chinese abroad have come to resent policies of the People's Republic which make it necessary for recipients to convert their remittances into specified kinds and quantities of goods at officially controlled rates. The shops in Hong Kong engaged in selling and shipping food parcels at fixed, expensive prices are part of the Communist plan to earn the maximum in foreign exchange through remittances. The scheme is quite simple and lucrative. A person in Hong Kong merely orders a package of food to be delivered to relatives in China. Net profits from the sale and shipment of the food go into Peking's foreign-currency balance to be used in purchasing needed goods abroad. Anybody who has seen the long, patient queues of Hong Kong people outside the designated shops knows the plan is successful simply because other ways of sending remittances are difficult or uncertain.

In addition to the inadvertent or intentional Communist curbs on remittances, there are the obstacles erected by the foreign-exchange controls of the various places where the overseas Chinese are established. In some countries, the transfer of funds can be legally accomplished; in others—for example, the United States—it is unlawful to remit to the People's Republic. Nowhere, however, can currency controls be fully effective. Black-market or circuitous routes, notably through Hong Kong, are open to all.

The chief consequence of the official efforts of foreign governments to limit the availability of or deny their currencies to Communist China has been the creation of doubts about the size of the current flow of remittances. So many transactions are disguised that precise figures on the role of remittances in the international earnings of the People's Republic are not to be had. There is consensus among students of the problem, however, that remittances are declining.[5] This development is to be attributed to the ever more slender tie between the overseas Chinese and China. Under present conditions of isolation, there will be virtually no overseas settlers with close relatives on the mainland within another generation. The end of remittances may one day conclusively signal the fact that the overseas Chinese have all been born in their countries of residence.

The Emergence of a New Elite among the Overseas Chinese

The unprecedented isolation of the overseas Chinese and the changes it engenders appear to be bringing into being a new type of leadership in the communities of the settlers. Possibly some

[5] In a masterful and unaccountably unpublished survey, "Remittances to Communist China," Wu Chun-shi reports a 25 per cent decline in remittances to the mainland since 1950.

years must pass before this trend can be systematically examined through research, yet it is not too early to speculate that the overseas elite is coming to be constituted and recognized in new ways. A brief backward glance at the influential men of earlier times may suggest contrasts with present-day leaders.

During the centuries before the rise of nationalism, the elites of the overseas Chinese were normally either affluent or in command of powerful associations, notably the secret societies. Some leaders, of course, qualified in both respects. In many areas, the governing authorities granted titles and perquisites to Chinese leaders in an effort to use these notables as instruments for control of the general Chinese population. It seems clear, however, that administrative dignity was bestowed only on men already prominent, although the officially recognized Chinese leader was customarily able to augment his fortune and prestige through licensed participation in state monopolies over opium, pawnshops, gambling, or markets. Until the close of the nineteenth century, then, overseas Chinese communal dignitaries were respected for their riches, their command over the activities of the associations, and, to a degree, their closeness to the officialdom.

That the elite standing of these men among their compatriots was enhanced by their links with colonial administrators resulted from a tendency of the overseas Chinese to lean toward the center of power. Such an inclination is, of course, typical of apprehensive minorities. Jews in Slavic parts of the Hapsburg empire were likely to favor Austrian culture and the German language; Indians in Kenya gravitated toward the British, not the Africans.

In the present century, different measures of elite status came to be applied. Attachment to the culture of China and involvement, usually financial, in Chinese national endeavors became essential for those aspiring to influence and high social position. By and large, leaders continued to be drawn from the ranks of the rich, but the associational credentials demanded for power in the twentieth century were of a new sort. As pan-Chinese organizations gained in strength and popularity over narrowly based kinship, territorial, or occupational associations, the elite came to be composed of men regarded as broad in perspective and profound in their sense of duty. Dedication to community goals and to the strengthening and elevation of China became their hallmarks. It was no longer adequate to be the chief of a strong clan association. Ruling a secret society became disreputable. Too intimate or dependent a connection with the colonial administration was likely to be a liability.

The path to leadership was to be found in working for the realization of Chinese national objectives. For example, the chambers of commerce and the schools of the overseas Chinese in Southeast Asia were major agencies for nationalist mobilization, and office in a chamber or on a school board signified community leadership. By the late 1930s, efforts to raise money to underwrite local community enterprises or, more politically significant at the time, to aid the Chinese state and people with disaster relief or gifts of military equipment flourished throughout the overseas Chinese world, and those who directed these activities also enjoyed elite status.

Under such circumstances, leadership roles became attainable for some men who were not renowned for their wealth. Newspaper editors and school principals, as the nationalistic vanguard, were naturally in respected positions. It must be remembered, however, that such members of the elite ultimately depended upon the financial backing of the owners of their papers and the trustees of their schools. Until World War II, the overseas elite continued to be composed largely of and dominated entirely by wealthy men who differed only in their nationalism from the leaders of the nineteenth century. The difference was certainly great, but even more profound changes were to come in the postwar period.

Since the war and more especially since 1949, the display by members of the overseas elite of attachment to China has been vastly more difficult and complicated than in previous times. Most leaders have had to shy away from involvement in the politics of China. In some countries, open support for the Communists is banned; elsewhere, working for the Nationalists is prohibited. Sympathy for either side cannot be blatantly displayed in Malaysia and Singapore. Even where such political expressions are tolerated, deep entanglement in the affairs of a Chinese regime is regarded as unwise. The bulk of the overseas elite have attempted to maintain their nationalistic images and still avoid specific political identification. The task has been hard for some, impossible for others. As examples of the fate of leaders too intimately linked to a Chinese party, one can cite the cases of conspicuous Kuomintang supporters forced to leave Indonesia or of the late Tan Kah Kee, the most eminent Singapore leader, who concluded that his commitment to China obliged him to live out his final years in the People's Republic.

The extremes of deportation to Taiwan or residence on the mainland have obviously been chosen by few. Leaders in the Chinese communities of Southeast Asia have necessarily been required to adjust to situations in which open participation in the politics of either Chinese regime is at best ill advised. Increasingly and inevitably, the elites of the isolated overseas Chinese have turned their faces toward local problems and policies. (In fact, leaders and followers alike have reoriented themselves toward Southeast Asia as concern for their immediate environment has become paramount. While twenty-five years ago one could correctly view the Chinese of the area as almost uniformly detached from the political lives of their places of residence, a striking reversal has since taken place.)

The new overseas Chinese leadership, only now taking shape, is less and less concerned with establishing reputations as men devoted to China. The emphasis of these men is on guiding their compatriots toward the best possible accommodation within the societies and states of Southeast Asia. Such a course can cause the elite to seek to put the overseas Chinese in securely privileged positions in the area, but the attempt is made within a Southeast Asian context and with the means locally available. Outside support from a Chinese government is not the basis of the drive. In this redirection of loyalties and revision of methods, the emerging elite differs from the old and from the Communist competition.

To understand the character of the emerging elite, it is important to remember that the techniques of promoting overseas Chinese ends within the Southeast Asian context have undergone and are undergoing change. In colonial times, the Chinese typically found themselves in a middle position in societies stratified in three levels. The Westerners were on top, and the indigenous masses were at the bottom. The obvious and exploited method for winning Chinese advances lay in alliance, usually tacit, with the alien rulers. Economically, the Chinese and the Westerners had complementary roles. Politically, the two elements shared faith in the necessity for law, order, and effective administration. The Chinese most wanted license to pursue their individual and communal goals; colonial administrators were quite content to permit the Chinese to develop autonomously so long as no danger to political stability arose.

In Singapore and Malaya late in the nineteenth century, the British felt strong enough and sufficiently threatened by the power of the secret societies to initiate efforts to bring the brotherhoods to heel. Before that time, there had been good reason to wonder whether British or clandestine Chinese power was paramount. In the same years across the straits in the Dutch colonies, the government felt obliged to enforce restrictions on Chinese travel and residence in order to protect Indonesians against Chinese exploitation which might breed unrest among the peasantry. Earlier, of course, when Chinese strength had seemed capable of challenging Western prestige, authority, or security, colonial regimes had on occasion reacted forcefully and sometimes, as in the Batavia and Manila massacres of the early colonial period, violently. Far more often than not, however, the administrative reward for cooperation in colonial rule and economic development was considerable communal freedom for the Chinese.

Greater bargaining power was available to the settlers when, in the first decade of this century, Chinese nationalism became a force. Overseas Chinese appeals to the symbol and the state of China irritated and frightened Western administrators. No colonial government in Southeast Asia in the period before the emergence of Chinese nationalism had undertaken to provide the overseas Chinese with education, social welfare, or entry into official careers. These opportunities and services came only when the total rendering of overseas Chinese allegiance to China and the consequent intervention of the Chinese state in Southeast Asian affairs seemed the only alternatives. Under such circumstances, it was feared, the Chinese in the colonies would prove unmanageable, and the indigenous population would cease to be awed by Western imperial splendor. Moreover, the Western powers would suffer diplomatic embarrassment in international affairs in dealing with one another and, more ominously, with Japan.

The colonial authorities granted concessions to the overseas Chinese, but at the same time they sought to check Chinese nationalism. The founding of Chinese consulates in Southeast Asia was resisted, and once they were established, attempts were made to circumscribe their operations. Chinese political movements were universally suspect. In Malaya, the British eventually felt compelled to outlaw the Kuomintang as prejudicial to their sovereignty and, not at all incidentally, obstructive to the placation of Japan.

At present, with colonialism gone and Communist China currently unwilling to lend open, regular support to overseas Chinese causes, the settlers abroad must adjust to the consequences of their own isolation in post-revolutionary Southeast Asia. No longer can they hope to take advantage of the apprehensions and weaknesses of an alien regime. Except for Malaysia, there are now no plural social and political orders to be kept in balance with Chinese cooperation. The indigenous peoples and their rulers are joined by their common ethnic heritage and their nationalism. Unification, not division, is the goal and the basis of the regimes of independent Southeast Asia. Chinese separateness, once politically protective, has become a handicap. The need to find means to fit into the present-day scheme is recognized by all. Disagreement arises only over methods. There seem to be three basic ways for the settlers to react—to remain aloof from Southeast Asian politics, to seek political assimilation in their overseas homelands, or to follow the path of communalism, including the Communist variety.

Detachment from their political environment is of course feasible for the Chinese abroad only in a relative sense. Even attempts to minimize involvement and contact with Southeast Asian officials represent a form of negative political action, a difficult form at that. Only under unusual circumstances are the Chinese permitted the luxury of relative political isolation. The case of South Vietnam comes to mind as unique. There the settlers are concentrated in self-contained urban centers, most massively and notably in Cholon, the Chinese sub-city of Saigon. The inhabitants there are engaged to a remarkable degree in providing goods and services for themselves and maintain fewer daily ties with non-Chinese than is essential and customary for Chinese settlers elsewhere. As a result, the Vietnamese authorities have legislated on such matters as citizenship and the language to be used in public but have generally been content to leave Cholon and its lesser counterparts to themselves. The tendency is of course strengthened by the fact that recent South Vietnamese governments have been unable to look beyond immediate threats to their own survival.

In the rest of Southeast Asia, only individual overseas Chinese, not whole communities, can attempt non-involvement in politics. It makes no fundamental difference whether Chinese politicization leads to open party activity, to clandestine treachery, or to under-the-counter payments to influence indigenous holders of authority. All such activities, in a broad and real sense, are political. Clearly, many—probably most—settlers would be happier to be left alone, but in the politically vibrant countries of the region, swiftly changing conditions demand a Chinese response. Education, citizenship, and economic opportunity are universal concerns. Action in these areas can come only from or through governmental agencies. The pattern of efforts to secure favorable or tolerable treatment from the state varies from country to country in accordance with the political climate of the time and place. In Singapore, where the Chinese have direct, popular control over a democratic government, ballots are decisive. In Malaysia, the enfranchised settlers seek to safeguard their interests with their votes and, at the party level, through an alliance with the politically dominant Malays. Elsewhere, the Chinese and their communal representatives can attempt to serve their ends through cooperation with the indigenous elites either in the form of open support, as was the case of the pro-Sukarno Baperki, or through the bribery that is widely endemic.

The emerging leadership of the overseas Chinese thus seeks to meet and deal with the current rulers of Southeast Asia. The task requires skills and attitudes of a kind largely unknown among earlier Chinese leaders. Language is of prime importance. The nationalist rulers of the area quite reasonably demand a willingness among the Chinese elite to break away from the common haughtiness of the colonial past which discouraged use, at least educated use, of indigenous languages. Today's Chinese communal spokesmen are generally expected to be linguistically compatible with the officialdom of their countries of residence. Malaysia and the Philippines are rather special in that English continues to be respectable, but this linguistic legacy from colonial times may evaporate. The old-style leader could get by with colonial administrators in some ungrammatical and debased Western or local language. Indeed, the literature suggests that colonialists viewed such linguistic impurity as quaint and symbolically humble. At present, however, government officials in Southeast Asia are offended by failure to use nationalistically acceptable language.

The need for learning a language is part of a broadened insistence upon education as the basis for elite status. Chinese leaders in a less complicated age could rely on the prestige of wealth. Today the semi-literate *nouveau riche* is passing from the ranks of leadership. As Southeast Asia won independence and sought development and as Chinese society there has sunk deeper roots, professional positions formerly so largely held by Westerners have been opened to Asians. With their running start in education, some Chinese have moved into the gap. While in the first twentieth-century decades the respected members of an overseas community were rich merchants who embraced Chinese nationalism to add to their stature and influence, physicians, lawyers, editors, labor union officers, teachers, industrialists, traders, and career politicians are currently pushing aside the old leadership. Men of the new breed share an intellectual attachment to progress and the realization that the attainment of their goals, both individual and communal, is compatible with and dependent upon the advance of their Southeast Asian countries. Although naturally inclined to seek security for their fellow overseas Chinese, these men do not wish to preserve outdated exclusiveness and isolation.

Beyond the hopeless course of seeking to withdraw politically and the optimistic attempt to respond positively to the realities of post-colonial Southeast Asia, there is a third path open to the overseas Chinese—communalism, especially in its modern form, communism. The Chinese Communist effort in the region seems to represent a strange and sinister blend of the communal separateness of colonial times and the political activism of the present. Like the political assimilationist above ground, the Communist leader is a man of the modern world concerned with material advance; but after the example of the obscurantists of the prewar Chinese elite, the Communist is bred in communalism and nurtured in chauvinism. Perhaps it is altogether fitting that these latter-day Marxists should be the products of a sort of dialectic.

If it is true or likely that the revolutions of Southeast Asia and the current isolation from China of the settlers are bringing the overseas Chinese to follow the emerging leadership along the road to political assimilation, then the remnants of the old communal elite will soon die out, not to be succeeded, and the Communist chauvinists will be passed by. The danger lies in the possibility that there will be no opportunity for the new assimilationist leadership to form and take command. Because of the longevity of traditions of communalism, the transfer of leadership from the old-style narrow nationalists to the new, more complex, Southeast Asia-oriented elites can be neither easy nor unopposed. The extremists of the left and of the right both have vested interests in the survival of communalism. There are, however, credible reasons to hope for the political assimilation of the overseas Chinese.

Prospects for Political Assimilation

The time is now propitious for the Chinese of Southeast Asia to reassess their position. One of three courses must be followed. As was indicated in the discussion of leadership, the settlers can decide on non-involvement, communalism, or political assimilation. It is not unreasonable to suggest that political assimilation has grown more attractive and feasible in recent years. Under colonialism, separateness was politically useful and socially desirable. Assimilation to the indigenous political culture before independence would have cost the Chinese their political bargaining weapons and their prestige on the middle rung of the social ladder. The top position occupied by the colonialists would of course have been beyond the grasp of more than a token few. Today moving into indigenous circles will not bring political impotence and lowered status; on the contrary, the local nationalist elites command power and respect. Particularly in Thailand and Malaysia, the Chinese are moving toward greater political participation, although the patterns in the two countries are individually quite distinctive.

The developments in Thailand involve the process of absorption, so it is appropriate to make a few general and preliminary remarks on this subject with respect to Southeast Asia as a whole. Burma, Laos, Cambodia, to some extent Vietnam, and most notably Thailand have long been remarkable for the relative ease with which members of the Chinese minority have been absorbed into the majority populations. The absence of religious barriers to intermarriage between indigenous Buddhists and Chinese settlers has been of central significance in this regard. Marriages between Chinese immigrants and local women, of course, do not necessarily produce assimilated progeny, but the children of mixed unions can reasonably be assumed to be more disposed toward assimilation than are those born of two Chinese parents.

Outside the Buddhist countries, few places in Southeast Asia have offered the Chinese much opportunity to disappear as an ethnic group. Although miscegenation has occurred throughout the region, presumably since the first Chinese arrived, culture and more especially and specifically religion have limited the process in the maritime countries. In the Catholic Philippines and even more in Indonesia and Malaysia, intermarriage has in the past century been rather exceptional, although it is now reported to be growing more common. It is true that vast numbers of Filipinos have Chinese forebears and that many of the older Chinese families in Indonesia and Malaysia are partly non-Chinese in ancestry. But the Chinese and indigenous populations in these countries maintained their identities with considerable sharpness, and when large-scale immigration of Chinese women began in the nineteenth century, interracial unions became less common.

Indonesia is now ahead of Malaysia in the acceleration of intermarriage. On the Malayan peninsula, the firm Islamic faith of the Malays limits mixed marriages; but observation indicates that where religion is not an obstacle, intermarriage is not unusual. For example, in interior regions in Sarawak, Chinese-Dayak couples are fairly numerous.

Twelve per cent of the marriages of Chinese in Indonesia are now supposedly mixed. The partners in these Sino-Indonesian unions typically are from the extremes of their social orders. Persons of high status can presumably afford to seek compatible mates without great concern for communal prejudices. Also, where the local people are firmly in political command, as always in Thailand and now everywhere, some Chinese may view marriage to an indigenous partner as both respectable and rewarding. Those from the bottom of the social order similarly, but for quite different reasons, are little inclined to be racially haughty in the matter of marriage as they must find partners where they can. Chinese families have traditionally sought to protect themselves by not letting children marry beneath them, and marriage to a local person has often been looked upon as socially degrading. Communal endogamy has thus been encouraged for the majority of the Chinese who are socially middle class in fact or at least in aspiration.

In Thailand, the descendants of Sino-Thai marriages have been able to fit into Thai society with striking success. So impressive is the record of assimilation of the Sino-Thais that the chief authority on the Chinese of Thailand, G. William Skinner, believes that the melting pot of Thailand has boiled, while that of America, by comparison, has merely simmered.[6] It is undeniable that acculturation and assimilation are sought and achieved by second- and third-generation Chinese settlers. Chinese family names, those most treasured and sacred symbols of Chinese identity, are regularly replaced by Thai surnames. Nothing could more convincingly prove the fact of Chinese absorption.

It may not be wholly idle to speculate at this point that as Thailand was never under colonialism, the Chinese there were better able to move toward assimilation. That is, because the Thai elite possessed power and commanded respect, the Chinese were not obliged as in a colony to seek strength through separation. Alliance with the indigenous people, not efforts to occupy the middle position in a plural society, permitted the Chinese to advance themselves. In other words, the Chinese of Thailand have always lived under the political and social circumstances that are just now

---

[6] A summary of this thesis is presented in G. William Skinner, "Change and Persistence in Chinese Culture Overseas," *Journal of the South Seas Society,* no. 16, 1960, pp. 86–100.

tending to favor trends toward Chinese assimilation in recently independent countries.

A recent statement by a prominent Sino-Thai sums up much of what is happening:

Speaking for those who are, like myself, partly Chinese, I should say first that we have never been to China. We don't know Chinese. We owe our allegiance to Thailand. But there are still those Chinese who have not been admitted to Thai citizenship. I don't know if your figure of four million is accurate: I would place it closer to one or two million. Most members of this group also consider themselves Thai even though they are essentially second-class citizens. But when you talk in terms of such large numbers it is impossible to make any sweeping statements. It would perhaps be safe to say that some are still taught to look to China at least as their father if not in fact their mother country. However, both Chiang Kai-shek and the Chinese Communists claim their allegiance. One good thing about the Chinese Communist regime is that many of the Chinese aliens in Thailand are no longer really alien. The wealthy Chinese especially dare not leave Thailand at the present time to visit China for fear of not being able to return. This makes the process of assimilation much easier.[7]

Malaysia has been quite different from Thailand with respect to the process of accommodating Chinese residents within the political system. Full assimilation along Thai lines has been blocked by the infrequency of Sino-Malay intermarriage. As a consequence, political assimilation has been the only path open.

Thus far, Malaysia's record of progress justifies hope. Indeed, most of the optimism in this brief study is derived from the postwar experience in Malaysia and Singapore. There is sound justification, however, for the use of that experience in the assessment of the Chinese abroad. Malaysia and Singapore have 25 per cent of Southeast Asia's Chinese, and, more impressive, Singapore alone contains a tenth of the world's overseas Chinese. By any measure, such percentages represent exciting and serviceable statistical samples. To be sure, no one can argue that what has happened in Malaysia and Singapore is necessarily taking place in other countries as well, for circumstances elsewhere are not identical. Nevertheless, it would be meaningless to attempt an ap-

[7] Alexandra Close, "Interview with Mr. Puey Ungphakorn, Governor of the Bank of Thailand," *Far Eastern Economic Review*, v. 48, no. 8, May 20, 1965, p. 356.

praisal of the Southeast Asian Chinese without giving Malaysia and Singapore paramount attention. In addition, the Chinese there have been uniquely tested by Chinese Communist insurrection and by participation in democratic elections and parliamentary government. It is in Malaysia and Singapore that the new Chinese leadership oriented toward Southeast Asia is conspicuous and that the settlers have thus far rejected political withdrawal and Chinese chauvinism. The pages to follow, then, will stress lessons from Malaysia and Singapore; but stress is not overemphasis.

The campaign of Communist terrorism, the Emergency, has been portrayed both as a contest between Chinese and non-Chinese in Malaya and as a fight between communism and colonialism. There is truth in these two interpretations, but the story is more complex and richer than such simple accounts suggest. For the Chinese settlers, the Emergency was a test of their commitment to their adopted homeland. The Communists for reasons of political expediency and orthodoxy sought to present their movement as a multinational endeavor in which Chinese, Malays, and Indians participated, oblivious to differences of ancestry and culture. In fact, as was known by all, the Communist attempt at revolution was Chinese in inspiration, leadership, and manpower. The existence of a sprinkling of non-Chinese in the movement received play in propaganda, but nobody seems to have been fooled into believing that the terrorists represented anything other than Chinese communism and chauvinism. Thus, from the point of view of the Chinese populace, the Emergency called for a decision between political attachment to Malaya or separation and extreme communalism.

The Communists had planned on winning support and weakening their enemies during an initial period of terrorism to be followed by guerrilla warfare fought from secure territorial bases. Final conquest would come, as actually happened in China, when the Communists moved into the cities and established a people's republic. The strategy was a faithful, flawless adaptation of the military doctrines of Mao Tse-tung to a colonial setting, but the plan did not work. The failure of the Communists must be attributed primarily and substantially to the unwillingness of the bulk of the Chinese in Malaya to support the campaign. The phase of terrorism instead of merely being introductory was to continue throughout the Emergency and eventually flicker out. The Communists never had enough popular or territorial support to move from terrorism to expanding guerrilla operations.

The plans of the terrorists rested upon the expectation that manpower and supplies would come from the Chinese community, and insofar as the Communist forces were replenished, the expectation was justified. It must be added, however, that the Chinese civilians were by no means generous and enthusiastic suppliers of men and goods. The Communists never managed to have more than 10,000 to 12,000 men in the field, and austerity, even hunger, was the lot of the jungle terrorist. The fact that the Communists were so often obliged to employ threats and violence to secure cooperation from civilian compatriots was symptomatic of weakness. The British did all they could to starve out the terrorists, but the primary usefulness of such police efforts seems to have been in making it safer for the civilians to resist Communist demands.

To cut the terrorists off from their chief channel of supply, the British eventually put into operation plans for the resettlement of Malaya's so-called Chinese squatters. Most of this group had established themselves on unused public land on the edges of the jungle during the Japanese occupation, when wartime economic stagnation had forced them out of the cities, mines, and rubber estates. The pattern was ideally suited to the Communist scheme. During the war, squatters helped resistance fighters, and during the Emergency, the terrorists counted on similar support. Specifically, the terrorists hoped that their couriers would be able to slip supplies and intelligence to them via the squatters and that the squatters would provide them with the food required for subsistence in the jungles. The British decision to deny the terrorists their main link with the outside and their source of food was thus inescapable. Implementing the decision, however, was an ambitious undertaking. More than half a million people had to be moved to safe and supervised locations, called "new villages," where the authorities provided housing, land, and protection. Nevertheless, the resettlement was executed smoothly, and the anticipated weakening of the terrorists was achieved.

Had the squatters fought resettlement, the program might have failed. In any case, massive resistance by the rural Chinese would surely have forced the British to transfer great numbers of security force personnel from combat to guard duty in the new villages; and, far more dangerous politically, squatters who perished in resisting relocation would have been held up as martyrs in the struggle against colonialism. The military and political repercussions of squatter intransigence might well have doomed the British to disaster.

The cities during the Emergency seemed oddly quiet. Even in Singapore, where three-fourths of the population was Chinese, there was no terrorism. The Communists had, of course, not planned urban violence as part of their early campaign, yet it is remarkable that the safest places in the country were where the urbanized Chinese were concentrated. No exercise of the imagination is required to see that the defeat of the terrorists would have been made immeasurably more costly had the British been compelled to station sizable security forces in the cities to guard against terrorism there. Even isolated and infrequent violence in the cities would have drawn government troops and police away from the main theater of combat in and around the jungles.

It can be submitted that the majority of the Chinese in Malaya deserve major credit for the checking of the Communists in that country. A British victory against unified Chinese popular resistance would have been at best pyrrhic. To date, study of the politics of the Emergency has been shockingly neglected. Few developments in the history of Southeast Asia, indeed in recent global history, can be regarded as more decisive. In Asia, Malaya was the scene of a major Communist failure and the only country where a Chinese population successfully turned against Chinese communism. The British military role need not be underplayed in recognizing the Chinese political contribution. Perhaps the thesis to be tested through future study is that in Malaya British soldiers won the battles while Chinese civilians won the war.

Developments leading to the independence of Malaya and the subsequent establishment of Malaysia further tested the political orientation of the Chinese. Surely, neither the British nor the Malays could have supported the end of colonial rule on the peninsula in 1957, when the Emergency had not yet evaporated, had there been doubt as to the reliability of the Chinese population. The bringing together in the Alliance of the major Malay, Indian, and Chinese parties was evidence of the absence of irreconcilable communalism. To be sure, the leaders of the three cooperating parties have continued efforts to safeguard the special concerns of the communities represented in the Alliance. On the other hand, consensus has been achieved on shared national goals, and an effective balance of interests has been maintained with considerable success. Outside the Alliance, the extremes of the Chinese left and Malay right on the Malayan peninsula are splinters capable of causing infection but not of assuming power.

It cannot be denied, of course, that the Malays have been jealous guardians of the political paramountcy which they enjoy as the result of constitutional and electoral provisions favorable to their community. Nor should one forget that the indigenously based component of the Alliance, the United Malays National Organization (UMNO), has its own right wing of vocal, anti-Chinese politicians capable of stirring mob passions. Furthermore, the current arrangement providing for Malay political domination and Chinese economic control cannot be permanent. Malay economic aspirations will rise, and the number of Chinese voters will grow as the franchise is extended through naturalization and the attainment of voting age by those who are born citizens. The fabric of the Alliance may therefore grow fragile in years to come; but for the present, the system works.

Although Singapore was part of Malaysia for less than two years, the willingness of Malaya to have Singapore join in an expanded federation in 1963 was interpreted to mean that the Chinese were recognized as trustworthy. Of course, it must be admitted that the Malays reportedly feared that Singapore, if excluded from Malaysia, might degenerate into a city-state under Chinese Communist domination. Furthermore, the Malays believed that they could remain politically dominant in the new federation. Sarawak and North Borneo, now Sabah, were included in it in part to give it a majority of non-Chinese peoples. Beyond this safeguard, the Malays counted on statutory provisions agreed upon in writing and in advance. Even with these qualifications, however, it remains true that Singapore's entry into Malaysia symbolized a measure of faith in the ability and desire of the Chinese there to be constructive citizens. That the plan failed does not mean that it was naïve in concept.

Within Singapore during the period of preparation for Malaysia's formation, there developed a contest between the Chinese chauvinists and those who sought political incorporation in the planned state. The political assimilationists were represented by the People's Action Party (PAP) under the leadership of Lee Kuan Yew, an eminent example of the emerging overseas Chinese elite. The chauvinists, some of whom have been charged with Communist subversion, found their means of political expression through a leftist offshoot of Lee Kuan Yew's party called the Barisan Sosialis. (The name is a Malay term meaning "socialist front.") The line between the two sides was thus unmistakably defined, and the struggle between the People's Action Party and the Barisan Sosialis was to confirm the relative weakness and the divisions of the Chinese extremists in the most Chinese city of Southeast Asia.

The campaign in Singapore built up in intensity over many months. Basically, the Barisan sought to make the Chinese fear Malaysia and to cause the Malays on the peninsula to dread Singapore's inclusion in the proposed federation. The PAP, on the other hand, attempted to convince the Chinese of the need for Malaysia in order to assure independence from colonialism and continued economic progress and to publicize the protection which constitutional safeguards written into the Malaysia agreement provided for Chinese voting rights and education and for the labor movement in Singapore. Both sides were industrious in their propaganda efforts. The PAP made full use of the communications facilities available to it as the governing party; the Barisan carried out a house-to-house campaign. Reports circulated that Barisan activists planted rather fanciful rumors in the packed neighborhoods of the Chinese working class and among the relatively less articulate rural Chinese of the island state. They are said to have warned, for example, that Malaysia would bring Muslim rule to Singapore and that as a result the eating of pork, the favorite meat of the Chinese, would be prohibited. The most imaginative rumor reported claimed that the Muslims ruling Malaysia would insist on circumcision as a prerequisite for citizenship. On a more sophisticated level, the Barisan condemned Malaysia as an anti-Chinese, neo-colonial plot.

The Barisan appeal to Chinese chauvinism and, less importantly, to doctrinaire socialism appeared ominously powerful to many observers, including the present writer, at the time. In retrospect, it seems that the Barisan made two serious blunders. First, it failed to recognize the futility of an appeal to intense Chinese nationalism which would isolate Singapore and leave the island politically precarious and economically moribund. Second, it confused the voters by at first supporting the complete merger of Singapore and Malaya under Barisan terms and by later instructing followers to cast blank ballots in the referendum in which voting was compulsory and rejection of the Malaysia plan was impossible. The first maneuver was patently designed to frighten the Malayan government at Kuala Lumpur into backing out of the Malaysia scheme; the second aimed at embarrassing the PAP. Had there been a majority of blank ballots, Barisan demands for a general election might well have been irresistible.

On the day of the referendum, September 1, 1962, the Singaporean Chinese proved themselves. Seventy-one per cent of the electorate endorsed the PAP-supported proposal for Singapore to enter Malaysia under terms preserving the island's authority in the vital areas of citizenship, education, and labor legislation. The other two choices offered the voters on the ballot were almost totally ignored. Only one-fourth of the electorate decided to declare itself for the Barisan by casting blank ballots. The PAP had swept the field with what must be interpreted as an appeal to the Chinese of Singapore to place their own local interests above Chinese nationalism and separatist communalism.

The battle was not ended with the referendum. The PAP and the Barisan were to challenge one another for months in preparation for the general election held on September 21, 1963. The basic contest between orientation toward Malaysia and Chinese chauvinism remained central and generated the bitterness of the campaign. Lee Kuan Yew denounced the Barisan members as at best dupes of the Communists; in racist response, Barisan people were heard to taunt the Singapore prime minister by calling him "Harry" Lee, the name he had used as a student at Cambridge, and to accuse him of selling out to the British and the Malays. All other issues were insignificantly peripheral.

When the votes were counted in 1963, the PAP had won an enormous, but by no means unqualified, victory. The electorate had empowered Lee Kuan Yew to continue as prime minister of Singapore in command of 37 out of the 51 seats in the Assembly. The Barisan won 13 seats, while a splinter party got the remaining one. Examination of the popular vote for the PAP, as contrasted with the tally of triumphs in the 51 single-member constituencies, reveals that the Barisan was merely defeated, not destroyed. The PAP won a plurality of 47 per cent of the total votes cast, but the Barisan picked up a substantial 33 per cent. It is noteworthy that support for Malaysia and for the pragmatic socialism of Lee Kuan Yew was weakest in the rural districts of the island which are heavily Chinese peasant in population, while with two exceptions the urban workers' constituencies rejected the Barisan.[8]

The explanation of Barisan strength in the rural areas is presumably to be found in two situations. First, the rural Chinese had become upset over the actions and plans of the PAP government to carry out programs of residential and industrial development which threatened their farms. Second, the rural people appear to be rather poorly fitted into the multinational society of Singapore. They are less likely to be in daily contact with non-Chinese Singaporeans; more decisive, they are not direct participants in the economic life of the great international emporium. As a result, they can be regarded as a generation behind their urban fellows in terms of shaking off the compulsions of Chinese nationalism and responding to new leadership. This argument is admittedly far from systematically tested, yet it offers an interpretation of Singapore voting patterns which is worth consideration.

Despite the ragged edges of the PAP electoral success, September 1963 was a turning point. A numerous Chinese electorate was allowed to express itself through secret, honestly counted ballots. At no other time or place have Chinese voters received such a democratic opportunity to go on record on the funda-

[8] Milton E. Osborne, *Singapore and Malaysia*, Data Paper No. 53, Southeast Asia Program (Ithaca, N.Y.: Cornell University, Southeast Asia Program, July 1964), *passim*.

mental issue of their loyalty. The lesson of the Singapore election may well indicate the nature of the reorientation of the overseas Chinese toward Southeast Asian problems and solutions that is in process.

As is well known, when Malaysia came into being in mid-September 1963, Sukarno ordered his open attack on the new federation. Indonesia proclaimed a policy of "confrontation" against Malaysia and justified it by Sukarno's professed fear of encirclement by neo-colonialist forces. The Indonesian president involved the Chinese of Malaysia in the contest in two contradictory ways. For consumption by Western diplomats and anti-Chinese Southeast Asian nationalists, Sukarno presented his policy of confrontation as a defense against the spread farther southward of Chinese Communist power. To the Chinese in the region and on the China mainland, Sukarno addressed the claim that his "crush Malaysia" drive aimed at destroying neo-colonialism and bringing about true liberation for his exploited neighbors. Peking reacted with warmth to the latter explanation of Jakarta's purposes. Any move hostile to the Western presence in Southeast Asia inevitably serves Communist China's grand strategy. In one of Peking's recent and rare messages to the overseas Chinese, it urged the Chinese of Malaysia to combat the neo-colonial oppression under which they suffer. It is probably unnecessary to add that no mainland publications for the same period carried a similar call for a rising by the Chinese in countries such as Indonesia, which were by Peking's definition liberated and friendly.

In Malaysia itself, the Chinese population at large did not seek to sabotage their new country. Opposition to the federation was the stand of the Barisan in Singapore, the far left in Malaya, and militant Chinese chauvinists in Sarawak; but no large-scale local Chinese hostility made the task of containing Indonesian infiltrators markedly tougher for the security forces. Even more than during the Emergency, disloyalty among the Chinese was uncommon, except perhaps in Sarawak.

If Sukarno's plot to kill Malaysia in its infancy was based in part on an expectation of substantial assistance from a Chinese fifth column, he must have had to re-examine his war plans. Indonesian confrontation, if anything, seemed to mobilize the peoples of Malaysia. Of all the countries of Southeast Asia, Indonesia has been the most brutal toward the overseas Chinese; and this record was thoroughly familiar to the Chinese of Malaysia, many of whom have personal and business links with Indonesia. Although Sukarno is acknowledged by the Chinese in his own country to have intervened on their behalf to check army plans for an anti-Chinese pogrom, it would have been a triumph of the imagination to come up with a name less appealing to most Malaysian Chinese than that of the Indonesian president. It may not be off the mark to argue that Sukarno, in his negative fashion, helped bring the Malaysian Chinese to the support of Kuala Lumpur. The suggestion has been offered, at least in the form of a quip, that the federation's government ought properly to erect a statue to Sukarno as the person who did the most to unite the diverse peoples and interests of Malaysia.

It has to be recognized, of course, that the authorities were vigilant in efforts to prevent the formation of subversive forces in Malaysia. Suspects were arrested and detained; special emergency powers were granted the police. Just as the skill of Lee Kuan Yew was helpful in leading Singapore into Malaysia, efficient law enforcement facilitated the control of subversion. The Barisan Sosialis was crippled by the Singapore authorities, but that challenge to Malaysia has been severely dealt with by the voters before major blows were struck by the police. A dramatic and convincing event shortly after the general election further marked the decline of the extreme left in Singapore. In October 1963, the anti-Malaysian leaders on the island sought to organize a general strike of political protest. The attempt was a humiliating failure. An insufficient number of workers went on strike, and the planned show of force became a symbol of the collapse of the chauvinists. Preventive security measures by the authorities, then, were useful, not decisive. The power of the officials would have counted for little if it had not rested on a base of popular support.

In another and far more peaceful sphere, the Singapore Chinese were, and still are, also establishing their attachment to their Southeast Asian home. Not because of pressure from the government but because of the spontaneous decisions of the citizenry, fewer than half the Chinese children on the island now attend Chinese-language schools. To anybody acquainted with the twentieth-century history of the Chinese abroad, this development is phenomenal. Overseas Chinese nationalism has centered on education. The Chinese school systems of Southeast Asia were the pride and hope of the overseas nationalists, and enormous sums of money have been donated to support them. Official control over Chinese education has been resented and fought throughout the region. It is not farfetched to argue that without the educational issue and the indoctrination accomplished in the Chinese schools, overseas nationalism would have been a feeble thing. Yet, at present, a majority of Chinese parents in Singapore have chosen English schooling for their children. Not long ago, parents exposed themselves to social censure if they opted for non-Chinese education and thus had their children grow up alien to Chinese culture and intellectually dependent upon foreigners.

Several considerations have prompted the educational shift. English is no longer the language of colonial rulers and is thereby politically clean. In business and in government, English is the vehicle of men in power. English, of course, comes closer than any other language to being a world language, and Singaporeans are very much part of the international scene. Finally and crucially, the English-language schools of Singapore have been free of the political agitation that has gripped Chinese schools. Many parents reportedly have jusified the denial of Chinese education to their children on the ground that they were thus seeking to save their children from dangerous political involvement. Whatever their motivations, the Chinese parents of Singapore are engaged in a quiet revolution. When one considers that in the past the line dividing political assimilationists from Chinese chauvinists has largely coincided with the line separating the English-educated from the Chinese-educated, the implications of Singapore's break with the past may well prove momentous.[9]

[9] In an enlightening article, Wolfgang Franke argues that Chinese education per se does not breed political rebelliousness. Instead, the disaffection of the Chinese-educated in Singapore arises after graduation when they discover that their diplomas open few doors to employment. See "Chinese into Ma-

Despite progress after 1963, political infighting between Lee Kuan Yew and the Alliance led to justified fear that Malaysia would fall apart. There could be no gainsaying the fact that Lee was treading on sensitive toes. It was also true that the leadership of UMNO had been shocked and offended by their losses to the PAP in Malay constituencies in Singapore in 1963 and by the PAP electoral invasion, albeit abortive, of the peninsula the following year. Nevertheless, it seemed impossible to conclude, although some perceptive pessimists did so, that the PAP or the Alliance sought to tear Malaysia into pieces. A few months before the Singapore-Malaysian break, an editorial in a journal deserving respect seemed to put the case most effectively:

It may appear incongruous to draw attention to the progress and achievements of Malaysia at a time when Kuala Lumpur and Singapore are at each other's throats. . . . [The dispute] has now escalated into a larger squabble involving all the economic, political, racial, and commercial pressures which are at present putting relations between the island and the Capital under strain.

But both the Tunku and Lee Kuan-yew are eminently sensible men and both realize what they stand to lose by allowing the rift to widen beyond repair. If left to their own devices, the two men would undoubtedly achieve a working arrangement; but unfortunately both are under pressure which prevents this: the Tunku from the right-wing, obscurantist politicians who represent anti-Chinese racialist tendencies within the Alliance, and Lee Kuan-yew from the Singapore left wing. But the extremist dangers have been removed: the Communists have been effectively dealt with in Singapore, while last February's arrests of right-wing plotters who planned to set up a government in exile in Karachi have drawn the teeth of the most dangerous pro-Indonesian minority in Malaya.[10]

The August 1965 split between Singapore and what remains of Malaysia did, however, take place. Perhaps at first it seemed to be the result of the failure of the large overseas Chinese population of the city-state to assimilate politically. To be more precise, it may have appeared to stem from an enduring Chinese attachment to old patterns of communalism and chauvinism and an unwillingness to seek political accommodation within a Southeast Asian context.

---

laysians," *Far Eastern Economic Review*, v. 47, no. 10, March 12, 1965, pp. 460–461.
[10] "Under Pressure," same, v. 48, no. 4, April 22, 1965, p. 147.

A diametrically opposed analysis, however, makes more sense. Singapore was indigestible within Malaysia precisely because its leaders sought to operate on a national, multicommunal plane and to make full use of the local political weapons at hand. Had Lee Kuan Yew been content to be the spokesman for a single ethnic group in his home city, after the example of old-style leaders, Singapore would still be in Malaysia. Driven by the circumstances of his time and, of course, by his personal ambition as a rising politician, Lee moved onto the national stage. Although his actions may have been overly bold, they were fully rational, for Lee is a master craftsman sensitive to political currents.

Far from advocating Chinese domination of Malaysia, Lee Kuan Yew sought to change existing patterns of communalism. Lee recognized that overseas Chinese interests would thus be served, but his primary concern appears to have been the implementation of his brand of democratic socialism. The formula for change was tidily expressed in the call for a "Malaysian Malaysia." The emphasis was on equality for all citizens and for all states in the country. Had Lee's dream materialized, the special rights of the Malays would no doubt have been whittled away. Correspondingly, Singapore would have gained full parliamentary representation in Kuala Lumpur. In these senses, a "Malaysian Malaysia" would have strengthened the urban, Chinese moderate left, but such developments were to come through parliamentary and constitutional compromise. The isolation of Singapore from the rest of Malaysia was the last thing Lee wanted.

The leaders of the dominant Malay party, UMNO, and their conservative Chinese allies within the ruling Alliance were horrified. Every move by the Singapore prime minister, whether in his party's all but totally unrewarding campaign in parliamentary constituencies on the peninsula or in his efforts to form political ties with similarly restless men in Penang, Malacca, and the Borneo states, bred resentment in Kuala Lumpur. Finally, the prime minister of the central government of Malaysia invited Singapore to secede. Lee Kuan Yew had made himself politically insufferable because he was an active political assimilationist. A communal separatist might have fared better.

It is instructive to recall at this point that Singapore's independence is limited both in scope and in spirit. Politically, Lee Kuan Yew and his electorate remain essentially assimilationist. Not desiring to commit economic suicide, Singapore hopes to continue to serve Malaysia as a great entrepôt. The Singapore government continues to persist in efforts to promote the use of Malay as an official language. Finally, Singapore decided to commit troops to Malaysian defense even after the split with Kuala Lumpur. This act, more than anything else, symbolized the continuation of much of the pre-secession status quo.

Singapore had hoped at the time of secession that trade with Indonesia would be resumed, but Sukarno's embargo was only gradually lifted. The only immediate commercial gain Singapore enjoyed after it was set adrift politically came from the cancellation of orders for the closing of the city's branch of the Bank of China. The Singapore authorities insist that the bank will have to be purely commercial in its operations and not function as a political agency of Peking. Whether such purity can be preserved, of course, remains to be seen. In any case, it is undeniable that many Singapore firms, especially those of modest size, are relieved that an inexpensive source of credit is not to be dried up.

Finally, it is useful to remember that Lee Kuan Yew appeared profoundly saddened when secession came and that he has since voiced the hope that Singapore can re-enter Malaysia in ten years or so. In the latter regard, the Singapore prime minister may well envisage a future when the Chinese electorate on the peninsula will have grown sufficiently to erode Malay communal strength and bring a shift to the left. Lee may even look to the passing of the old guard of the Alliance. If so, he can be charged with no more than political ambition. He remains spokesman for a fundamentally assimilationist overseas Chinese public.

This essay has laid heavy stress on Malaysia and Singapore as the fulcra of overseas Chinese politics. Perhaps this emphasis results simply from the wish of a chronically optimistic writer to find signs of health in an afflicted part of the world; yet the discovery of parallels between Malaysia and Singapore and other countries may suggest that the former are merely different, not unique, and that there are general trends toward political assimilation throughout the overseas Chinese world.

In this regard, developments among the overseas Chinese in

Indonesia merit attention. With the addition of some observations about the Indonesian scene, the essay will have considered signs of assimilation among 10 million, or 80 per cent, of the 12 million or so overseas Chinese of Southeast Asia, for it has already touched upon the long history of Chinese assimilation and absorption in Thailand and upon the trends toward political assimilation in Malaysia and Singapore. Therefore, there would seem to be no pressing need to try to assemble evidence from additional countries.

There can be no doubt that a growing proportion of the numerically great Chinese population of Indonesia has been headed in an assimilationist direction. The long-standing bifurcation of the overseas Chinese in the archipelago into those locally oriented on the one hand and those emotionally tied to China on the other has been reinforced by citizenship laws. If, as Donald Willmott has estimated,[11] there are about one million alien Chinese in Indonesia, there are more than half again as many Chinese bearing Indonesian citizenship.

The one million aliens are isolated from open participation in Indonesian politics. Their children attend special schools. Restrictions imposed on their economic activities decrease their opportunities for interaction with ethnic Indonesians. In other words, partly through their own choice and partly because of pressures from the authorities, the aliens are bound by communal separatism.

The 1.7 million or so locally rooted Chinese with Indonesian citizenship have been moving away from the aliens. There is no Chinese education for the children of Indonesian citizens, regardless of ancestry. Despite governmental efforts to promote the economic rise of indigenous Indonesians, in part at the expense of citizens of alien ancestry, the Chinese citizens of the island republic operate in a wide circle of economic activity. Significantly, such men come into close contact with the government and with ethnic Indonesian colleagues, competitors, customers, employers, and employees.

At the political level, Indonesian citizens of Chinese origin

[11] Donald E. Willmott, *The National Status of the Chinese in Indonesia, 1900–1958* (Rev. ed.; Ithaca, N.Y.: Cornell University, Modern Indonesia Project, 1961), p. 69.

sought through their mass organization, Baperki, to participate in Sukarno's "guided democracy." Baperki, of course, did not operate as a political party in normal parliamentary and electoral senses. Such conduct would have been inappropriate and indeed impossible in a political society where the emphasis was on the maintenance of balance among contending forces, interests, and functional groups. Sukarno as the keystone of that equilibrium and as a friend of the assimilationists held Baperki's loyalty.

Thus, the separatists and the assimilationists among the Chinese in Indonesia have been divided. They do not share a common leadership; their aspirations are mutually antagonistic. Moreover, the split continues and can be expected to widen if the political assimilationists move toward the achievement of their goal of final and full acceptance as Indonesians.

A hasty word of caution must be added. Two dangers to Chinese assimilation in Indonesia may lurk in the future. The triumph, now apparently forestalled, of a Communist party closely allied to Peking might make retention or acquisition of Chinese identity attractive and expedient. A new form of Chinese separatism might facilitate riding a surging Communist tide. More significant at the moment, the ascendancy of anti-Communist military leaders could similarly thwart political assimilation, for the Indonesian army has long been regarded as unfriendly to the local Chinese, regardless of citizenship. Military rule might well drive those who are currently assimilationist into the cramped, insecure haven of communalism. In Indonesia, as events since October 1965 show, almost anything can happen.

Threats to Political Assimilation

Lest it be charged that the hopeful forecast implied here is blindly naïve, it must be acknowledged that among the Chinese of Southeast Asia there is ignorance, opportunism, violence, and treachery. Communalism, left and right, lives on. It would be misleading and foolhardy to ignore the dangers on the path toward the peaceful assimilation of the Chinese within the political societies of the region. Therefore, a closer look at the black spots on the recent record of the Chinese themselves is necessary.

As has previously been noted, the chief Chinese foes of assimilation are on the right and on the left, but there are also some essentially apolitical saboteurs. The right includes old-style community leaders and Kuomintang diplomats and stalwarts who are understandably distressed at the prospect of a loss of Chinese identity by the settlers. So much sacrifice and toil have gone into the effort to build Chinese nationalism among the overseas people that the opposition of the builders to demolition is to be anticipated. The passing leadership, at best guilty of cultural haughtiness, cannot accept gracefully the decline of Chinese separatism. Not only do these men fear their own loss of influence; they loathe the thought of fading communalism. They are not necessarily attached to a political cause, but those who are Kuomintang men are doubly disturbed. Just as a Kuomintang return from Taiwan to the mainland remains a comforting dream, so the hope survives that the backing of millions of Chinese abroad will increase the prestige and might of the Nationalists.

The peril to political assimilation from the right is compounded by the willingness of some indigenous nationalists to enter into tacit alliance with the Chinese communalists in order to keep alive the overseas Chinese scapegoat. The rewards to be won by local political opportunists are twofold: the Chinese right-wing leaders are invitingly easy marks for extortion, and administrative and policy failures can be explained away as the result of Chinese betrayal.

The secret societies and other criminal organizations constitute a sinister source of trouble. Having in the decades of nationalism degenerated into bands of hoodlums, the Chinese secret societies are capable of appalling savagery. The criminal brotherhoods were deeply implicated in the September 1964 Chinese-Malay rioting in Singapore. Apparently, the instigators of that fighting were Malay thugs, but their Chinese colleagues in crime soon counterattacked. It would be more than a little enlightening to learn the motivation of the professional criminals for their involvement. As an underworld gang, after all, is normally a business enterprise, it seems logical to suspect that the society members were hired to increase intercommunal violence. The identity of the murderers' employers, however, remains hidden.

(An earlier explosion between Chinese and Malays in Singapore in July 1964 was less complex in its origins. It is reported that the first blows were struck by Malays. The Chinese simply retaliated later. The main lessons in Singapore's grisly record of rioting in 1964 are that at no time were whole communities engaged in battle and that neither of the periods of street fighting is to be blamed on popular Chinese communal separatism. Singapore's riots dramatized most cruelly the strains of building a multinational political order, but they did not seem to signal a halt to political assimilation.)

The Communists are the third and gravest threat to political assimilation. The motives of the young Chinese in Southeast Asia who enlist in the Communist movement are presumably far from simple. The willingness of a person to elect a life of danger and discipline can never be easily explained. Lucian Pye's sharp insights into the pattern of Chinese Communist recruitment and organization during the Malayan Emergency [12] reveal that ideology played a secondary role in attracting followers. The young terrorists seem initially to have sought companionship, a sense of purpose, a medium for the expression of idealism, and answers to the social and political problems around them. Moreover, the "Chineseness" of the conspiracy must not be overlooked as a source of appeal. The Communist recruits were attracted in fundamentally the same manner in which their elders had earlier been attracted to the Kuomintang. The differences between the Nationalists of the interwar decades and the Communists of the postwar years, in other words, lie in their use of members after enrollment, not in the nature of their recruitment processes.

There is no reason to assume that circumstances are much changed at present. Apprentices to communism are still found among the Chinese-educated youth. In Sarawak, the band officially designated the Clandestine Communist Organization is strikingly similar in personnel to that of the terrorists of the Malayan Emer-

[12] Lucian W. Pye, *Guerrilla Communism in Malaya* (Princeton University Press, 1956).

gency. An outsider is hard put to account for the readiness of young Malaysian Chinese to submit themselves to the rigors of training for jungle warfare. That the training is conducted in Indonesia makes the flow of volunteers seem even stranger, for Sukarno is not widely regarded as a friend of overseas Chinese communalism. The phenomenon can best be explained in terms of the power of Chinese chauvinism.

Roughly one-third of Sarawak's population is Chinese, and the other inhabitants belong to several different ethnic groups. There can be no overlooking the fact that the Chinese there are impressively productive. Indeed, Sarawak could never have entered upon the world economic stage without the Chinese. It is also true, from the Chinese viewpoint, that the indigenous cultures of Sarawak appear primitive. Pride of race is likely to be especially vigorous among Sarawakian Chinese, and their recent experience as pioneers in a raw land no doubt strengthens their enthusiasm. Thus, it is not surprising that Chinese chauvinism can be virulent in Sarawak. In this as in other matters, the Borneo state seems years behind Singapore and Malaya. If nothing else, the contrast between the Malaysian assimilationists and the Communist separatists highlights the heterogeneity of the overseas Chinese.

To the extent that national bigotry is the basis of existence for both the right and the far left of the overseas Chinese, it can be said that the Communist appeal is no less reactionary than that of separatist notions of ethnic superiority left over from prewar years. Under close scrutiny, the underground in Sarawak, the terrorist remnants on the Malayan peninsula, and the pro-Peking militants wherever they exist among the overseas Chinese surely seem driven primarily by chauvinism, not ideology. The chauvinism of the Communists perhaps justifies hope for the years ahead. As an essentially reactionary force, extreme Chinese nationalism in Southeast Asia must contend with the developing power of the assimilationist leadership, to say nothing of doing battle with indigenous nationalism in the area. The old right wing of the Chinese expatriates seems to have outlived its vigor and to be in irreversible decline. The future may well deal as mercilessly with the chauvinistic left. The Southeast Asia-oriented Chinese and their new leadership may not get the time they need to triumph over chauvinism, yet their success so far gives rise to an optimism that is a luxury in today's tropical Far East.

In conclusion, it is appropriate to add that the trend toward political assimilation was recognized by the late dean of the students of the overseas Chinese, Victor Purcell, who concluded his new edition of *The Chinese in Southeast Asia* with the following:

The main obstacle to the finding of a *modus vivendi* between the Overseas Chinese and the other races was the continuance of the Cold War. If the artificial alignment of humanity consequent upon this could be removed, it was likely that the presence of Overseas Chinese in Southeast Asia would become increasingly less a "problem." [13]

Reference to the global contest for political ascendancy leads the discussion at last to the role of the United States in overseas Chinese affairs.

[13] Victor Purcell, *The Chinese in Southeast Asia* (2d ed.; London: Oxford University Press, 1965), p. 568.

CHAPTER SIX

American Policy and the Overseas Chinese

Overshadowing all international tensions and disputes in Southeast Asia is the antagonism between the People's Republic of China and the United States. Barring foreign invasion and occupation, the futures of the countries of the region will primarily be shaped by internal forces, such as those stimulating trends toward overseas Chinese assimilation; but it is also true that no international event can now be wholly divorced from the Sino-American confrontation. Great or trivial, peaceful or belligerent, every exchange between the countries of the area appears ultimately related to the dominant contest. It makes no difference whether the issue is the pacification of South Vietnam, the viability of Laos, Sukarno's gyrations, or the title to a jungle ruin on the Thai-Cambodian frontier. Somehow China and America are, or seem to be, involved. The fundamental difference between the tactics of the two absentee giants arises from the simple fact that Washington stands to gain the most in a stable region, while Peking can operate best in turmoil. The actions and the fate of the overseas Chinese are influential here.

The recent history of Indonesian-Malaysian confrontation is particularly illustrative of the place of the overseas Chinese in the power politics of Southeast Asia. Sukarno sought to appeal to anti-Sinicism among the Filipinos and the Malays and at the same time to rely for anti-Malaysian support on the chauvinism of the Chinese extreme left in Malaysia, especially in Sarawak. To the indigenous peoples of the Malay peninsula and the Indonesian and

Philippine archipelagoes, Malaysia, when Singapore was still included, could be portrayed as a Chinese dagger thrust into the Malay world. Somehow, the hand grasping the dagger was identified as Anglo-American and neo-colonial. For its part, the overseas Chinese left was encouraged to believe that Malaysia was a plot to maintain the Malays in a position of political paramountcy in a country where the Chinese had a slight demographic plurality. Again, the villain behind the scenes was alleged to be Western neo-colonialism. In both these contradictory interpretations of the nature of Malaysia, it must be stressed, the overseas Chinese figured prominently.

Peking backing for *konfrontasi* may not have gone much beyond the broadcast of strident propaganda and some arms aid, but Communist China's endorsement of Sukarno's campaign in itself drew the overseas Chinese more deeply into the struggle. Before its recent adversity, the Indonesian Communist Party (PKI) was most vociferous in condemning Malaysia. That the PKI and Peking were joined in the anti-Malaysian effort implicated the overseas Chinese of Indonesia most dangerously. When the army began to seek the destruction of the PKI after the abortive coup of October 1965, the Chinese in the country were vulnerable to attack. Indeed, hostility to communism soon took the form of anti-Chinese activity by anti-PKI Muslims and others. Even the fundamentally assimilationist Baperki organization experienced violence. The Singapore cynics who say that anti-communism can most readily be expressed by anti-Sinicism seem to be correct. In Indonesia, the dangers to Chinese political assimilation and to social stability seem to have multiplied since the coup and counter-coup of early October 1965. Any American plan to support the foes of communism in Indonesia ought to rest on recognition of the long-range hazards of hostility to Chinese settlers in the islands.

To be more general, it can be suggested that the Southeast Asian Chinese can help secure the future of the region in two ways. First, the successful political assimilation of the settlers would of course erase the major and most widespread minority problem of the area. Second, the Chinese are superbly equipped to stimulate economic development vital to political health. Clearly, the Chinese cannot act alone in either respect. Encouragement from outside the Chinese communities will be needed, and the United States can seek to promote the extension of that encouragement. Therefore, some thoughts on possible opportunities for America can be offered. As the present course of U.S. policy toward the overseas Chinese in general favors their political assimilation, the suggestions to be presented will not be greatly at variance with ideas now influential in Washington. A hasty survey of the development of official American thinking on the overseas Chinese can serve as a preface to suggestions to follow.

The Evolution of American Policy

The triumph of the Communists on the China mainland in 1949 was not openly accepted as final by Washington. The denial of diplomatic recognition to Peking was symbolic of the state of the American official mind. Correspondingly, U.S. policy toward the overseas Chinese was for some years auxiliary to the war effort in Korea and to American support for the Nationalists on Taiwan. After peace was restored in Korea, the Taiwan Strait became the main theater of concern. Consequently, throughout the 1950s the preservation of overseas Chinese loyalty to the government on Taiwan was the goal of American actions—most notably in the work of the U.S. Information Agency. A most significant shift has come in the last few years because Washington has been drawn more and more deeply into Southeast Asia. The war in Vietnam, of course, is the focal point of that growing American involvement.

The southward reorientation of the United States' concern in Asia has produced a new determination to strengthen the non-Communist states of the region. Inevitably, American reliance on the fading promise of the Chinese Nationalists has declined. Thus, the overseas Chinese are now appropriately seen as more useful in the construction of strong Southeast Asian states than as supporters of the government on Taiwan. American policy toward Southeast Asia, favoring stability and national unity in the non-Communist countries, is of necessity broadly sympathetic to overseas

Chinese political assimilation, for Chinese communal separatism, even of an anti-Communist variety, no longer meets the established needs of Washington.

Opportunities for American Action

Although U.S. influence in the internal lives of the countries of Southeast Asia is restricted and uncertain, in some places virtually absent, there are opportunities for American action. Most simply, diplomatic suggestions to encourage the political assimilation of the overseas Chinese could be offered; but as unsolicited advice is unlikely to accomplish much and might well be resented, more ambitious efforts can be considered. For a start, Washington might try to persuade the Nationalists to ease up in their courting of the overseas Chinese, although the government on Taiwan is understandably reluctant to miss any chance to find strength. As was pointed out previously, the Chinese abroad are roughly equal in numbers to the population of the Nationalist island. Denied the hope of using the overseas Chinese as a reservoir of support, the Nationalists would suffer losses of both confidence and prestige. Actually, however, the Nationalists have already given token approval to the sinking of local roots abroad by Chinese settlers, and now is an appropriate time to make the approval meaningful. Continuation of separatist propaganda by Taipei seems likely to achieve two ends, both undesirable. As the appeal of the Nationalists is most hospitably received by older people, Taipei's work widens the gap between the generations of the overseas Chinese. Further and more dangerous, Nationalist propaganda naturally honors Chinese culture and thus could lay a foundation of chauvinism of possible use to the Communists.

Having presented the argument against Nationalist involvement in overseas Chinese affairs, one must record a reservation. It is a fact that the government on Taiwan serves as an alternative to that of the China mainland in attracting the loyalty of those Chinese abroad who do not yet display any orientation toward Southeast Asia. Therefore, there is the possibility that the eclipse of Taiwan would cause some overseas Chinese to redirect their emotions toward Communist China. Evidence and intuition suggest that the proportion of the Chinese abroad liable to be swayed from right to left by the dulling of the Nationalist symbol is small and likely to grow smaller as time passes. Nevertheless, the inconvenience to American policy in any increase in Southeast Asian support for Peking cannot be ignored.

Although specialists in the United States regard the suggestion as impractical and, as one official put it, "a can of worms," it is not outlandish to speculate that American aid programs in Southeast Asia could perhaps be designed in certain cases to promote the assimilation of the Chinese. Schemes encouraging economic co-operation and partnership between the Chinese and indigenous peoples at least merit thought. Admittedly, the implementation of aid policies along the lines proposed could invite indigenous suspicion and irritation; but the suggestions offered here do not call for crude, reckless schemes.

It might, for example, be feasible to devise means for the extension of loans on special terms to enterprises, large and small, operated multicommunally. Training programs for craftsmen and managers could be similarly devised to help break down ethnic exclusiveness in business. In the case of large construction projects, American aid administrators could seek to have the widest possible representation of the various ethnic groups in an area employed. Military aid seems especially adaptable to efforts to stimulate overseas Chinese assimilation. Wherever American assistance is accepted and militarily essential, there is an opportunity to urge that Chinese enter the armed forces for service and careers. The present writer most vividly remembers a conversation with a Bangkok Chinese who cited his past service in the Thai army as the chief reason for his identification with Thailand. The man's experience, of course, was not of American design, but it illustrates the role of army service in assimilation.

Finally, in the matter of economic development, the American government surely must avoid endorsing the economic nationalism of some Southeast Asian leaders. Hostility toward Chinese enterprise, after all, impedes general economic advance and works against the goals of programs for economic growth. The destruction of Chinese businesses would simply leave a vacuum which would be filled under most current circumstances by state enterprises. Presumably, Washington is not striving to promote state socialism. From the American viewpoint, Chinese prosperity can be regarded as proof of the productivity of free enterprise. The way to sell the system does not lie in attacks on its operators.

Education could become a major force in facilitating overseas Chinese assimilation. Expanded American aid could be invested in Southeast Asian institutions where Chinese and indigenous students alike are prepared for local careers. Grants could be made to support the publication of school texts designed to generate local loyalty; in fact, such efforts have been made by private American interests. Students from the region could be brought to the United States in increased numbers to receive advanced training. Graduates returning home would be likely to be committed to their professions and thus freed from narrow ethnic attachments. America has a vast and respected educational system, yet in terms of our resources, relatively little use has been made of education as an instrument of international politics. Other powers on both sides of the cold war have been more perceptive.

Philosophically and morally, education may perhaps seem sacrosanct; however, the proposal is not that opportunities for American training be held out as bribes to overseas Chinese youth, but that education be used in its proper and honorable role to produce men and women professionally dedicated and qualified. The example of the scholarships for students from China supported for many years by Boxer Indemnity funds could be a guide.

Many thousands of Southeast Asian students could be accommodated in the United States without great strain and at a cost modest in terms of foreign-aid expenditures. Obviously, the task would not be to make the students pro-American but to bring about their commitment to engineering, dentistry, literature, and all the other fields in which the new elites of Southeast Asia are to be found.

In these efforts to influence Southeast Asian political development, costly mistakes could be made. Simply stated, the danger is that American actions to push overseas Chinese assimilation through programs in aid and education might disastrously offend indigenous Southeast Asians and their governments. U.S. actions in these sensitive matters must be subtle and sophisticated. It is possible that the risks of stirring up indigenous annoyance may be too great to take. The question, in any event, deserves study.

Assessing the place of the U.S. Information Service (the overseas arm of the U.S. Information Agency) in this picture has not been easy. Opinions among specialists on Southeast Asia range from those of some American officials who state that USIS has been vastly influential and successful to those of a scholar convinced that the American information effort does far more harm than good. For the sake of the discussion here, let it be assumed that perhaps USIS operations in Southeast Asia could contribute to bridging the division between the Chinese and local peoples. Quite properly, USIS has made use of the example of Hawaii as an eminently successful experiment in multicommunal accommodation, although most Asians probably do not think Hawaii is truly part of the United States. Similar attention has appropriately been given to progress toward racial integration in mainland America. Such propaganda emphases make good sense, but USIS has not been unfailingly wise. With particular regard to the overseas Chinese, it seems that the American information program has made grave errors.

Any USIS effort to exploit among the Chinese abroad an emotional attachment to the Nationalists is a mistake. Attempts of this sort, if productive, can only serve to increase the communal separatism and political aloofness of the Chinese in their countries of residence. If such pro-Kuomintang messages are resented, then Washington has been made to appear foolishly reactionary. Yet USIS has served the Nationalists in both indirect and direct ways. There have, for example, been information releases which sought to advertise the value of American aid by presenting the genuinely admirable record of Taiwan's economic advance. It might be sounder to use only other Asian success stories to put across the message. Under necessarily unpublicized plans to support the Kuomintang, USIS has long run news services to provide copy for the pro-Nationalist press. It was formerly the practice to supply newsprint and subsidies to Kuomintang papers.[1]

---

[1] G. William Skinner, *Leadership and Power in the Chinese Community of Thailand* (Ithaca, N.Y.: Cornell University Press for the Association of Asian Studies, 1958), p. 136.

The use of the Chinese language in USIS publications is another error. Information ought to be presented only in English and the national languages of Southeast Asia. Printing in Chinese simply adds fuel to Chinese nationalism and chauvinism. Thus, there was no valid excuse for the operation of USIS special programs under so-called Chinese affairs officers. The danger that indigenous observers would be irritated by the policy was ignored. The present writer has heard Malays voice annoyance with a USIS vehicle put out in Singapore which all but ignores Malay in favor of Chinese and English. It must, in fairness, be assumed that such USIS encouragement of Chinese communalism is an honest, misguided act and not a deliberate move to divide peoples. Yet the official argument that the 125,000 copies of *The World Today* in Chinese distributed monthly by USIS have provided readers who know only Chinese with an escape from subscribing to Peking's propaganda is simply absurd. The USIS Chinese-language monthly circulates all but entirely in countries where Communist publications are banned. If *The World Today* suspended publication, its public could not, even if it tried, turn to the pages of the Peking *People's Daily* and *Red Flag*.

Finally, on the subject of American information programs, it needs to be added that enlightenment has begun to take hold. USIS, no longer blatantly pro-Nationalist as it was in the closing phase and the immediate aftermath of the Communist conquest of the mainland, now appears to support the assimilationist trend. Insofar as USIS uses the Chinese language as a medium of publication, assimilation is impeded; but American officials claim that there is no other way to reach segments of the overseas Chinese population. USIS seems to consider its Chinese-language service to be an expedient for the present likely to diminish in volume as assimilation progresses.

In summary, then, the focus of American officials concerned with political stability in Southeast Asia ought to be on fostering through assimilation a solution to what is known locally as the Chinese problem. Nothing the United States can do will in itself be decisive, but conscious, considered American efforts to support trends away from communalism should be made. The alternatives would seem to benefit Peking.

The Overseas Chinese and American Recognition of Communist China

The overseas Chinese frequently enter into discussion of an enduring feature of the Asian policy of the United States, the refusal to seek diplomatic relations with Communist China. Among the commonly cited justifications in the United States for nonrecognition of the People's Republic is the argument that the Chinese abroad would be swayed toward Peking by a change in American policy. There is evidence to support this assumption, although unless tested it cannot be accepted as conclusive. Perhaps it is appropriate to record here one man's speculation on the issue.

There would seem to be no reason to believe that the Chinese in Southeast Asia are particularly concerned with the American diplomatic snub. The attitudes of the settlers toward mainland China are shaped by factors close at hand; it is hard to imagine that a symbolic act in remote Washington could directly influence many. No doubt the prestige of the mainland regime would be enhanced by a gesture signifying final American acceptance of the reality of unchallenged Communist authority on the mainland; but those overseas Chinese eager to be impressed by Peking gains have already been thrilled by Chinese triumphs in warfare, power politics, and atomic research.

Rejection would be a most effective move for Peking to make in response to an American overture. The impact on the overseas Chinese of a refusal by the People's Republic to deal with Washington would be considerably greater than that of an acceptance. The Communists, by saying in effect that they would not be strengthened or dignified by U.S. recognition, would assert the brand of independence most admired by the chauvinists. Indeed, one of the best reasons for Washington to withhold recognition is that the offer might be turned down and thus give the People's Republic a new propaganda advantage. All in all, though, American decisions on recognition would not directly change many overseas Chinese minds; but the secondary consequences of a policy shift could be substantial.

Idle though the thought may be while war continues in Vietnam, it can be observed that if those Southeast Asian governments now diplomatically isolated from the People's Republic were to follow an American example of recognition, the lives of the overseas Chinese of Thailand, South Vietnam, the Philippines, Malaysia, and Singapore could be significantly altered. Obviously, the opening of Communist embassies in these countries would symbolize China's great-power status and perhaps suggest that the southward advance of Maoism would gain momentum. The jump of people on the political fence would then be fully predictable, but it surely cannot be assumed that most Chinese settlers are now politically passive and ready to swing to the Communists.

In the short run, the further opening of diplomatic relations between the governments of Southeast Asia and the People's Republic might actually favor the political assimilation of the overseas Chinese. Most notably in her relations with Indonesia, Communist China has shown a flexible willingness to avoid seeking to protect and manipulate the Chinese settlers when such acts appeared likely to endanger strategy dependent upon the cooperation of Southeast Asian leaders. It must be recognized, however, that Peking has acted out of expediency and could reverse its policy at will.

An outgrowth of Peking's current desire to be free of awkward entanglement with the Chinese abroad has been the campaign to urge settlers to acquire overseas citizenship. Emigrant sons in countries diplomatically recognized by the People's Republic are in effect told to secure naturalization and eliminate themselves as an international nuisance. In recent years, the open work of Communist Chinese embassies in Southeast Asia has seemed, as a worn cliché puts it, "correct." As there is no apparent likelihood that the policy will change in the near future, it can be assumed that Peking's diplomats will continue publicly calling for overseas Chinese assimilation. What will be done covertly is of course another matter, for Communist embassies might well seek secretly to exploit the overseas Chinese capacity for inviting resentment. Presumably, the determination of tactics would be based on conditions in each country. The fundamental question would be whether at a particular point Peking stood to gain more from promoting assimilation or from exacerbating intercommunal hostilities.

On one facet of the issue of American nonrecognition of the People's Republic there can be no doubt. There are those in Asia who suspect that the stand of the past sixteen, almost seventeen, years is not so much an expression of Washington's abhorrence of the brutalities of communism as a reflection of American racism. That is, some believe that the United States despises the men in Peking, not for their communism but because they are Chinese. Ridiculous though this belief is, it exists. Recognition of the mainland Chinese government would kill the suspicion and, in that way, put America in a more appealing light. But it must be emphasized that since the United States cannot hope to be more than vaguely influential in shaping the overseas Chinese future, whether or not it is admired will make slight difference.

Sorting out the likely effects of American diplomatic recognition of the People's Republic upon the overseas Chinese leads one to the conclusion that those who struggle with the issue need not be especially concerned with the reactions of the settlers. A variety of arguments for and against recognition can be raised, but it does not seem that the overseas Chinese response ought to figure prominently in any future thinking in Washington.

Summary and Conclusion

As this essay nears its close, it is appropriate to reaffirm the optimistic belief that the present offers the Chinese abroad unprecedented opportunities to escape their historic vulnerability. The path toward assimilation is opening. The end of colonialism broke down the social stratification which in the past barred Chinese entry into the top echelon of the Westerners and made the settlers fearful of sinking to the bottom stratum of the indigenous populations. The plural societies of colonial times have given way to evolving patterns of fluidity in which the Chinese can seek assimilation. Although ethnic and class animosities exist, the former racial bases of these evils do not seem to be present any longer. Rigid racial exclusiveness, elaborately and legally institutionalized, was brought to Asia by Westerners; now that the bearers of the white man's burden are subdued, it is highly possible that a more relaxed atmosphere will favor assimilation. Should the Chinese in independent Southeast Asia reject or be denied assimilation, the alternatives would be confinement in ghettos (at least figuratively), deportation, or worse.

The isolation from China of the overseas Chinese is the second and tremendously important factor promoting assimilation. Physically cut off from China by barriers to travel and migration, the settlers are obliged to take a fresh look at Southeast Asia. In a real sense, the Chinese abroad have finally accepted the notion that there can be no return to China. Actual repatriation was historically beyond the ability of millions, but repatriation as an ideal lived on. The overseas Chinese are only now making the psychological adjustment pressed on immigrants to the United States when they disembarked and cut the emotional tie with the ancestral country.

The communism of China has little in it to attract most of the Chinese abroad. A revolution capable of exploiting peasant unhappiness and nationalist frustrations can appeal to middle-class expatriates only through chauvinism, and the majority of the Chinese overseas are middle class, at least in aspiration. If it is true that Chinese chauvinism in Southeast Asia is outmoded and weakening, Maoism can be expected to enlist fewer and fewer followers in the region. Surely the domestic economic goals and political methods of the People's Republic are unlikely to win over many Chinese abroad. Contrary to a widely accepted interpretation, time may not be on Communist China's side. If the process of overseas Chinese assimilation moves ahead, their countries of residence will grow better able to stand on their feet. With no cheap victories to be had, Peking may become preoccupied with internal development and eventually grow comfortable enough at home to wish to avoid risks abroad. There is some encouragement in the fact that with the exception of the Korean War, Communist China has thus far cautiously held back from major, sustained, open conflict beyond her frontiers.

Unless a reversal of policy comes, the People's Republic is not prepared to intervene militarily in Southeast Asia simply to protect the region's Chinese. Just as the issue of American diplomatic recognition of Peking can be decided without direct concern for the overseas Chinese, the strategy of Communist China is not now shaped by that minority. Conceivably, a desire to protect the settlers could be used as an excuse for Chinese armed action, but the actual causes of such a move would be found elsewhere.

The reactions of the overseas Chinese to a Chinese invasion of Southeast Asia could probably be foretold. Given an opportunity, many would flee in keeping with the example of those Chinese who left North Vietnam to escape Communist rule. There would also be those who would serve as spies and saboteurs to support the advance of Chinese forces. Most Chinese settlers would, of course, merely seek to survive. The task would be difficult. The governments and peoples under attack in the region would no doubt deal harshly with Chinese residents.

If Chinese conquest were accomplished, the Communist authorities might prove equally unsympathetic. The overseas Chinese would not fit neatly into a Communist empire. Their history and economic strivings would make them troublesome. As Chinese, the expatriates could not be treated as a distinctive ethnic group to be permitted the trappings of national identity along lines established for the minorities of the People's Republic. Dispersed, the overseas people could not be governed in their own so-called autonomous region. The Chinese settlers under Communist occupation would at first probably be used but soon would have to be remolded. The process would entail suffering for many and regimentation for all. The economic virtues of the past would become sins. Separatism as an expression of national loyalty would become a vice. In a Communist Southeast Asia, the overseas Chinese could best serve the regime by minimizing friction between themselves and the indigenous peoples. To the extent that overseas chauvinism survived, the Chinese settlers would endanger the establishment of docile Communist colonies. Paradoxically, the Chinese of Southeast Asia might prove to be the most recalcitrant population in a conquered region. Peking could conclude that repatriation offered the most effective means of dealing with expatriate sons.

It is distressingly rare to end a discussion of Southeast Asia on a note of hope, yet there may be justification for doing so here. The overseas Chinese have not met the expectations of those who saw that minority as a dedicated and disciplined instrument for subversion. As study goes forward, the diversity and internal tensions fragmenting the settlers come to be recognized. The political assimilation of the Chinese is now feasible and in progress in most of the region. The pace of political assimilation is uneven, and the process will be lengthy. But the very existence of the trend was unimaginable in recent colonial times. The emerging assimilationist leadership, if given time, stands a chance. Reason would seem to be on the side of assimilation, although clearly man's history moves no more rationally than man himself.

The United States is obliged to do what it can to encourage assimilation, although it has to be recognized and re-emphasized that direct American influence on the overseas Chinese will be slight. For the Chinese, as well as for the other peoples of Southeast Asia, American support of those striving for independence and growth can be vital. Without that support, there can be only halting progress toward political maturity. The greatest American gift to the area would be time to seek solutions to internal difficulties. The overseas Chinese have much to contribute, but denied an opportunity, they cannot serve.

Selected Bibliography
of Works in English

Agpalo, Remigo E. *The Political Process and the Nationalization of the Retail Trade in the Philippines.* Quezon City: University of the Philippines, 1962. 344 p.

Alba, Victor. "The Chinese in Latin America," *The China Quarterly,* no. 5, January/March 1961, pp. 53–61.

Appleton, Sheldon. "Overseas Chinese and Economic Nationalization in the Philippines," *Journal of Asian Studies,* v. 19, no. 2, February 1960, pp. 151–161.

Barnett, A. Doak. *Communist China and Asia.* New York: Harper and Brothers for the Council on Foreign Relations, 1960. 575 p.

Campbell, P. C. *Chinese Coolie Emigration to Countries within the British Empire.* London: P. S. King and Son, 1923. 240 p.

Cator, W. J. *The Economic Position of the Chinese in Netherlands India.* University of Chicago Press, 1936. 264 p.

Chang-Rodriguez, Eugenio. "Chinese Labor Migration into Latin America in the Nineteenth Century," *Revista de Historica de America,* no. 46, December 1958, pp. 375–397.

Chen Ta. *Chinese Migrations, with Special Reference to Labor Conditions.* Washington, D.C.: GPO, 1923. 237 p.

———. *Emigrant Communities in South China.* New York: Institute of Pacific Relations, 1940. 287 p.

Comber, Leon. *Chinese Secret Societies in Malaya.* Locust Valley, N.Y.: J. J. Augustin, 1959. 324 p.

Coughlin, Richard J. *Double Identity, the Chinese in Modern Thailand.* Hong Kong University Press, 1960. 222 p.

Djamour, Judith. *Malay Kinship and Marriage in Singapore.* University of London, Athlone Press, 1959. 151 p.

Elliott, Alan J. A. *Chinese Spirit-Medium Cults in Singapore.* London: Royal Anthropolitical Institute for the London School of Economics and Political Science, 1955. 179 p.

Fall, Bernard. "Vietnam's Chinese Problem," *Far Eastern Survey,* v. 27, no. 5, May 1958, pp. 65–72.

Fitzgerald, C. P. "Overseas Chinese in South East Asia," *Australian Journal of Politics and History*, no. 8, May 1962, pp. 66–77.

————. *The Third China: The Chinese Communities in Southeast Asia*. Melbourne: F. W. Cheshire, 1965. 109 p.

Freedman, Maurice. *Chinese Family and Marriage in Singapore*. London: HMSO, 1957. 249 p.

————. "Chinese Kinship and Marriage in Early Singapore," *Journal of Southeast Asian History*, v. 3, no. 2, September 1962, pp. 65–73.

————. *The Chinese in South-East Asia: A Longer View*. China Society (London) Occasional Papers, no. 14. London: China Society, 1965. 24 p.

————. "Immigrants and Associations: Chinese in Nineteenth Century Singapore," *Comparative Studies in Society and History*, v. 3, no. 1, October 1960, pp. 25–48.

———— and Marjorie Topley. "Religion and Social Realignment among the Chinese in Singapore," *Journal of Asian Studies*, v. 21, no. 1, November 1961, pp. 3–23.

———— and William E. Willmott. "Recent Research and Racial Relations: South-East Asia, with Special Reference to the Chinese," *International Social Science Journal*, v. 23, no. 2, 1961, pp. 245–261.

Freyn, Hubert. "The Chinese in Thailand," *Far Eastern Economic Review*, v. 30, December 29, 1960, pp. 657–660.

Fried, Morton H., ed. *Colloquium on Overseas Chinese*. New York: Institute of Pacific Relations, 1958. 80 p.

Furnivall, J. S. *Netherlands India, a Study of Plural Economy*. New York: Macmillan, 1939. 502 p.

Golay, Frank H. "The Nature of Philippine Economic Nationalism," *Asia* (The Asia Society, New York), no. 1, Spring 1964, pp. 13–30.

Halpern, Joel M. "The Role of the Chinese in Lao Society," *Journal of the Siam Society*, v. 49, 1961, pp. 21–46.

Kahin, George McT. *Nationalism and Revolution in Indonesia*. Ithaca, N.Y.: Cornell University Press, 1952. 490 p.

Kaye, Barrington. *Upper Nankin Street, Singapore*. Singapore: University of Malaya Press, 1960. 439 p.

Kung, S. W. *Chinese in American Life*. Seattle: University of Washington Press, 1962. 352 p.

Landon, Kenneth P. *The Chinese in Thailand*. New York: Oxford, 1941. 310 p.

Lee, Rose Hum. *The Chinese in the United States of America*. Hong Kong University Press, 1960. 465 p.

Leigh, Michael B. *The Chinese Community of Sarawak*. Singapore:

Malaysia Publishing House for the University of Singapore, 1964. 68 p.

MacDougall, Colina. "The Chinese in Indonesia," *Far Eastern Economic Review*, v. 32, no. 8, 1961, pp. 361–365.

MacNair, H. F. *The Chinese Abroad*. Shanghai: Commercial Press, 1924. 340 p.

Mitchison, Lois. *The Overseas Chinese*. London: The Bodley Head, 1961. 93 p.

Murray, Douglas P. "Chinese Education in South-East Asia," *The China Quarterly*, no. 20, October/December 1964, pp. 67–95.

Newell, William H. *Treacherous River, A Study of Rural Chinese in North Malaya*. Kuala Lumpur: University of Malaya Press, 1962. 233 p.

Ng, Bickleen Fong. *The Chinese in New Zealand*. Hong Kong University Press, 1959. 146 p.

Osborne, Milton E. *Singapore and Malaysia*. Data Paper No. 53, Southeast Asia Program. Ithaca, N.Y.: Cornell University, Southeast Asia Program, July 1964. 115 p.

Parmer, J. Norman. *Colonial Labor Policy and Administration*. Locust Valley, N.Y.: J. J. Augustin, 1960. 294 p.

Png Poh Seng. "The Kuomintang in Malaya," *Journal of Southeast Asian History*, v. 2, no. 1, March 1961, pp. 1–32.

Purcell, Victor. *The Chinese in Malaya*. London: Oxford University Press, 1948. 327 p.

———. *The Chinese in Modern Malaya*. 2d rev. ed. Singapore: Donald Moore, 1960. 67 p.

———. *The Chinese in Southeast Asia*. 2d ed. London: Oxford University Press, 1965. 623 p.

Pye, Lucian W. *Guerrilla Communism in Malaya*. Princeton University Press, 1956. 369 p.

Robequain, Charles. *The Economic Development of French Indochina*. London: Oxford University Press, 1944. 400 p.

Silcock, T. H. and E. K. Fisk, eds. *The Political Economy of Independent Malaya*. Berkeley: University of California Press, 1963. 306 p.

Simoniya, N. A. *Overseas Chinese in Southeast Asia, A Russian Study*. Data Paper No. 45, Southeast Asia Program. Ithaca, N.Y.: Cornell University, Southeast Asia Program, December 1961. 151 p.

Skinner, G. William. "Change and Persistence in Chinese Culture Overseas: A Comparison of Thailand and Java," *Journal of the South Seas Society*, no. 16, 1960, pp. 86–100.

Skinner, G. William. *Chinese Society in Thailand*. Ithaca, N.Y.: Cornell University Press, 1957. 459 p.

————. *Leadership and Power in the Chinese Community of Thailand*. Ithaca, N.Y.: Cornell University Press for the Association of Asian Studies, 1958. 363 p.

Somers, Mary F. *Peranakan Chinese Politics in Indonesia*. Ithaca, N.Y.: Cornell University, Modern Indonesia Project, 1964. 56 p.

Song Ong Siang. *One Hundred Years History of the Chinese in Singapore*. London: Murray, 1923. 602 p.

Tan Giok-lan. *The Chinese of Sukabumi: A Study in Social and Cultural Accommodation*. Ithaca, N.Y.: Cornell University, Modern Indonesia Project, 1963. 314 p.

Thio, Eunice. "The Singapore Chinese Protectorate," *Journal of the South Seas Society*, no. 16, 1960, pp. 40–80.

Thompson, Virginia and Richard Adloff. *Minority Problems in Southeast Asia*. Stanford University Press, 1955. 295 p.

T'ien Ju-k'ang. *The Chinese of Sarawak*. London School of Economics, 1953. 88 p.

Uchida Naosaku. *The Overseas Chinese: A Bibliographical Essay*. Bibliographical Series No. 7, Hoover Institution on War, Revolution, and Peace. Stanford University, 1959. 134 p.

————. "Overseas Chinese Problems in Southeast Asian Nations," *Asian Affairs*, v. 5, no. 1, October 1960, pp. 71–81.

van der Kroef, Justus M. "Communism and Chinese Communalism in Sarawak," *The China Quarterly*, no. 20, October/December 1964, pp. 38–66.

————. "Nanyang University and the Dilemmas of Overseas Chinese Education," *The China Quarterly*, no. 20, October/December 1964, pp. 96–127.

Wang Gungwu. "The Chinese (and the Commonwealth) in Southeast Asia," *Commonwealth Journal*, no. 5, March/April 1962, pp. 85–90.

————, ed. *Malaysia*. New York: Praeger, 1964. 466 p.

————. *A Short History of the Nanyang Chinese*. Singapore: Donald Moore, 1959. 42 pp.

Weightman, George H. *The Philippine Chinese*. Ann Arbor, Michigan: University Microfilms, 1960. 478 p.

Wickberg, Edgar. *The Chinese in Philippine Life, 1850–1898*. New Haven: Yale University Press, 1965. 280 p.

————. "Early Chinese Economic Influence in the Philippines, 1850–1898," *Pacific Affairs*, no. 35, Fall 1962, pp. 275–285.

Williams, Lea E. "Chinese Entrepreneurs in Indonesia," *Explorations in Entrepreneurial History* (Harvard University), v. 5, no. 1, October 15, 1952, pp. 34–60.

———. "Chinese Leadership in Early British Singapore," *Asian Studies* (University of the Philippines), v. 2, no. 2, August 1964, pp. 170–179.

———. *Overseas Chinese Nationalism.* Glencoe, Ill.: Free Press, 1960. 235 p.

———. "Sino-Indonesian Diplomacy: A Study of Revolutionary International Politics," *The China Quarterly*, no. 11, July/September 1962, pp. 184–199.

Willmott, Donald E. *The Chinese of Semarang.* Ithaca, N.Y.: Cornell University Press, 1960. 374 p.

———. *The National Status of the Chinese in Indonesia, 1900–1958.* Rev. ed. Ithaca, N.Y.: Cornell University, Modern Indonesia Project, 1961. 139 p.

Wong, C. S. *A Gallery of Chinese Kapitans.* Singapore: Ministry of Culture, 1963. 114 p.

Wynne, Mervyn Llewelyn. *Triad and Tabut.* Singapore: Government Printing Office, 1941. 540 p.

Index

134 *Index*

COUNCIL ON FOREIGN RELATIONS

PUBLICATIONS

FOREIGN AFFAIRS (quarterly), edited by Hamilton Fish Armstrong. THE UNITED STATES IN WORLD AFFAIRS (annual). Volumes for 1931, 1932 and 1933, by Walter Lippmann and William O. Scroggs; for 1934–1935, 1936, 1937, 1938, 1939 and 1940, by Whitney H. Shepardson and William O. Scroggs; for 1945–1947, 1947–1948 and 1948–1949, by John C. Campbell; for 1949, 1950, 1951, 1952, 1953 and 1954, by Richard P. Stebbins; for 1955, by Hollis W. Barber; for 1956, 1957, 1958, 1959, 1960, 1961, 1962 and 1963, by Richard P. Stebbins; for 1964, by Jules Davids; for 1965 by Richard P. Stebbins.

DOCUMENTS ON AMERICAN FOREIGN RELATIONS (annual). Volume for 1952 edited by Clarence W. Baier and Richard P. Stebbins; for 1953 and 1954 edited by Peter V. Curl; for 1955, 1956, 1957, 1958 and 1959 edited by Paul E. Zinner; for 1960, 1961, 1962 and 1963 edited by Richard P. Stebbins; for 1964 by Jules Davids; for 1965 by Richard P. Stebbins.

POLITICAL HANDBOOK AND ATLAS OF THE WORLD (annual), edited by Walter H. Mallory.

ATLANTIC AGRICULTURAL UNITY: Is It Possible?, by John O. Coppock (1966).

TEST BAN AND DISARMAMENT: The Path of Negotiation, by Arthur H. Dean (1966).

COMMUNIST CHINA'S ECONOMIC GROWTH AND FOREIGN TRADE, by Alexander Eckstein (1966).

POLICIES TOWARD CHINA: Views from Six Continents, edited by A. M. Halpern (1966).

THE AMERICAN PEOPLE AND CHINA, by A. T. Steele (1966).

INTERNATIONAL POLITICAL COMMUNICATION, by W. Phillips Davison (1965).

MONETARY REFORM FOR THE WORLD ECONOMY, by Robert V. Roosa (1965).

AFRICAN BATTLELINE: American Policy Choices in Southern Africa, by Waldemar A. Nielsen (1965).

NATO IN TRANSITION: The Future of the Atlantic Alliance, by Timothy W. Stanley (1965).

THE ORGANIZATION OF AMERICAN STATES AND THE HEMISPHERE CRISIS, by John C. Dreier (1962).

THE UNITED NATIONS: Structure for Peace, by Ernest A. Gross (1962).

THE LONG POLAR WATCH: Canada and the Defense of North America, by Melvin Conant (1962).

ARMS AND POLITICS IN LATIN AMERICA (Revised Edition), by Edwin Lieuwen (1961).

THE FUTURE OF UNDERDEVELOPED COUNTRIES: Political Implications of Economic Development (Revised Edition), by Eugene Staley (1961).

SPAIN AND DEFENSE OF THE WEST: Ally and Liability, by Arthur P. Whitaker (1961).

SOCIAL CHANGE IN LATIN AMERICA TODAY: Its Implications for United States Policy, by Richard N. Adams, John P. Gillin, Allan R. Holmberg, Oscar Lewis, Richard W. Patch, and Charles W. Wagley (1961).

FOREIGN POLICY: THE NEXT PHASE: The 1960s (Revised Edition), by Thomas K. Finletter (1960).

DEFENSE OF THE MIDDLE EAST: Problems of American Policy (Revised Edition), by John C. Campbell (1960).

COMMUNIST CHINA AND ASIA: Challenge to American Policy, by A. Doak Barnett (1960).

FRANCE, TROUBLED ALLY: De Gaulle's Heritage and Prospects, by Edgar S. Furniss, Jr. (1960).

THE SCHUMAN PLAN: A Study in Economic Cooperation, 1950–1959, by William Diebold, Jr. (1959).

SOVIET ECONOMIC AID: The New Aid and Trade Policy in Underdeveloped Countries, by Joseph S. Berliner (1958).

NATO AND THE FUTURE OF EUROPE, by Ben T. Moore (1958).

INDIA AND AMERICA: A Study of Their Relations, by Phillips Talbot and S. L. Poplai (1958).

NUCLEAR WEAPONS AND FOREIGN POLICY, by Henry A. Kissinger (1957).

MOSCOW-PEKING AXIS: Strength and Strains, by Howard L. Boorman, Alexander Eckstein, Philip E. Mosley, and Benjamin Schwartz (1957).

RUSSIA AND AMERICA: Dangers and Prospects, by Henry L. Roberts (1956).